Endorsements

Ecclesiastes 3:1 tells us that there is a time for everything, and a season for every activity under the heavens; this is life, transitioning through a series of seasons where the Lord takes us from glory to glory, resembling Him in ever-increasing measure. Transitioning well, from the old season to the new is key and very much depends on our willingness to let go of the familiar and embrace the change. In Sweet Sorrow, Barbara gently and compassionately comes along side mothers who are attempting to adjust their sails to a new normal and leads them into the freedom to just BE whom the Lord has created them to be: a daughter of the King and the bride of Christ. The Lord has given Barbara a profound gift to see into the hearts and emotional struggles of women in order to bring them to a place of peace, value and wholeness.

I have deep respect and honor for mothers and the blood, sweat and tears they put into raising children and while it is true that raising children is a Kingdom advancing mandate from the Lord, mothers transitioning out of that season are not done. Rather, they have a brand-new place and purpose in the Kingdom of God that they must step into and fill for the advancement of the Lord's work. If you are in that place now, I strongly encourage you to pick up this little, but powerful book and allow the Holy Spirit to speak to you through its pages and reveal to you your Godly identity and next season.

Benjamin Deitrick, Founder
Ignite Ministries International

Barbara De Simon has a great sensitivity to God, family, and people in general. She also has an acute awareness of people in distress, including those experiencing the sweet sorrow of having invested much of their lives helping their children to mature into young adults, only to release them through marriage into the hands and hearts of someone who has only known their child for a few years.

I have great respect for Barbara as a mover and shaker in the Kingdom of God, but my highest regard for her centers on her love for God and people. Tears filled my eyes time and again as I read this book. I'm a father, not a mother, but my heart turned toward myself and my own children as I relived my experiences as a father, and for six years, a single parent with full custody of three children transitioning from adolescence to adulthood. Barbara's insight on the battles of physical and spiritual orphans is rich and enlightening.

Each chapter brought new revelation to me. After ministering deep healing and deliverance for over twenty years, I thought how *Sweet Sorrow* can reinforce everything people receive through such ministry and help them walk out their freedom.

I highly recommend this book for mothers and fathers, married and single parents, as well as every adult child. Sweet Sorrow will bless those who are strong in faith and those just beginning to develop their faith. Anyone who truly reads this book, reflects on it, and completes the exercises prescribed within will achieve greater self-awareness and victory by doing so.

Dr. Douglas E. Carr
Doug Carr Freedom Ministries Inc.

Editorial Review

Sweet Sorrow - Releasing Your Son to His Bride: What Every Mother Needs to Know is a work of non-fiction focusing on advice from a Christian standpoint and was penned by author Barbara De Simon. Written for mothers who need an emotionally supportive read to help them redefine their relationship with their sons once they leave and get married, the work takes us through an approach which encourages readers to trust in Christ at their sides to help guide them. This, when coupled with the sense of community and experiences of the author on the topic, produces a comprehensive overview of the emotions, thought processes and struggles that one can expect at this time.

Writing a specific kind of devotional work in order to guide people through this emotional journey is a really clever idea, and author Barbara De Simon has achieved it beautifully with her work. Where readers might struggle on their own to find the scriptures to help them, De Simon not only signposts the relevant material to provide Christian guidance but also talks through the quotes and explains examples to provide a deeper real-world context for mothers who are struggling to let go. The narrative reads in a friendly and compassionate tone whilst also delivering accuracy and confidence, making readers feel as though they're in safe and loving hands. Overall, Sweet Sorrow is an insightful read for any mother saying goodbye to her son and starting a new phase in her life: a highly recommended guidebook.

- K.C. Finn, Readers' Favorite, 5-Star Rating

Surviving the Emotional Waves of Releasing Your Son to His Bride

BARBARA DE SIMON

Copyright © 2020 2024 Barbara De Simon
Windsor, Ontario, Canada
Barbdesimon.com

All rights reserved. No part of this publication may be reproduced, distributed, or transmitted in any form or by any means, including photocopying, recording, or other electronic or mechanical methods, without the prior written permission of the author, except in the case of brief quotations embodied in critical reviews and certain other non-commercial uses permitted by copyright law.

Unless otherwise noted, scripture quotations are taken from *The Holy Bible*, New International Version®, NIV®, Copyright © 1973, 1978, 1984, 2011 by Biblica, Inc.™ Used by permission. All rights reserved worldwide.

Scripture quotations marked TPT are from *The Passion Translation*®. Copyright © 2017 by BroadStreet Publishing® Group, LLC. Used by permission. All rights reserved. thePassionTranslation.com.

Scripture quotations marked NLT are taken from *The Holy Bible*, New Living Translation, copyright © 1996, 2004, 2015 by Tyndale House Foundation. Used by permission of Tyndale House Publishers, Inc., Carol Stream, Illinois 60188. All rights reserved.

Scripture quotations marked AMP are taken from *The Amplified Bible*®, copyright © 1954, 1958, 1962, 1964, 1965, 1987 by The Lockman Foundation®. Used by permission of the Lockman Foundation and the Zondervan Corporation. All rights reserved.

Scripture quotations marked NKJV are taken from *The Holy Bible*, New King James Version®, copyright © 1982 by Thomas

ISBN: 978-1-7383840-0-6

Dedication

This book is dedicated to my three amazing sons: Jeremy, Gabriel and Jonathan of whom I am so very proud. I thank God for them all and trust that the Lord will lead them and guide them into His wonderful plan for their lives, as they surrender to Him.

Contents

Acknowledgements ~ 11
Introduction ~ 13
Part I ~ Experiencing the Waves ~ 19
Chapter 1 ~ Two Become One ~ 21
Chapter 2 ~ Relationship Over Religion ~ 27
Chapter 3 ~ Fully Immersed In Him ~ 35
Chapter 4 ~ A Road to Wholeness ~ 47
Part II ~ Surviving & Thriving ~ 53
Chapter 5 ~ From Orphan to Daughter ~ 55
Chapter 6 ~ From Daughter to Bride ~ 81
Chapter 7 ~ Emotional Attachments ~ 99
Chapter 8 ~ Bitter Judgements & Ungodly Promises ~ 107
Chapter 9 ~ Letting Go ~ 115
Chapter 10 ~ Prodigals ~ 127
Chapter 11 ~ Releasing and Sending ~ 131
Chapter 12 ~ What Now? ~ 135
Appendix A ~ 140
Appendix B ~ 144
Appendix C ~ 153
About the Author ~ 155
Bibliography ~ 156

Acknowledgements

I would like to acknowledge my God in heaven for leading me into this ministry and giving me the gifts to accomplish this work. I also would like to acknowledge my friend, Deborah Lovett, from Women Gathered and Women of the Well Ministries, for inspiring me to write this book, sharing her heart and spurring me on. As well, I would like to acknowledge my leaders and pastors at Shekinah Apostolic Equipping Center in Ann Arbor, Michigan: Apostle Barbara J. Yoder, Pastors Benjamin & Tarrah Deitrick, Pastor Bernardine Daniels and Deborah Combs for supporting me and pouring into me each week. In addition, a heart-felt *thank you* to Apostle Douglas Carr for his leadership and support.

Introduction

"One last push," was the nurse's order as the doctor put himself in the catcher's seat, perched between my knees. One last hurrah, one last breath sucked in and held, one last scream and there it was—fire! Fire where no one on God's green earth should ever feel fire. If you're nodding your head right now, you too, have birthed a child naturally. Congratulations and God bless you! You are part of the *holy mother of God that is painful* club! Whether or not you had a c-section or vaginal delivery, we have all known the joy of sharing the good news with everyone in sight and feeling your child kick and even hiccup inside your womb. It is a wonder and a miracle in every way!

I'm amazed and grateful as I look back to my early married years. There was a time when we weren't sure if we were going to be able to have our own children. We had been trying for over a year with no success—long white sticks, revealing only negative results laid waste in the garbage bin for many months. I found myself in a heap on the floor crying out to God in disappointment and desperation several times. Through it all, God was faithful as He led me to unravel some toxic emotions in my heart, forgive my mother, face some fears, renounce some lies and repent for some inner vows I had taken as a young teenager, in order to reproduce according to His plan and desire. How many of you know that God is all-powerful, but He can only do what you co-operate with, in all *three* parts of who you fully are—spirit, soul and body? God does not and will not trump our free will. He cannot do what you, *really deep down* don't want Him to do or aren't willing to receive. In the beginning, God chose to give us free will and now He honors our choice, though I love how He sways our hearts toward His own. "For it is God who works in you to will and to act according to his good purpose" (Phil. 2:13).

We now have four children, including twin boys, and our first two children are grown adults already. My, oh my, how time flies when you're having fun, running around trying to meet everyone's needs, juggling activities, roles, and responsibilities! I thank God every day for His goodness, mercy, and great faithfulness to us. My full story of overcoming temporary fertility challenges along with twenty-one steps to inner healing can be read in my book *Barren No More*, available on Amazon. For the reader who is not yet a mature Christian and is struggling with unexplained infertility, my book *Key to Fertility*, is also a great resource and encouragement. It too can be purchased on Amazon.

Our first-born blessing, Jessica, finally came into the world two and a half years after we first began trying to conceive, by c-section due to Placenta Previa. Our first-born son, Jeremy, who is also a blessing, was born on February 19, 1997, naturally—a vastly different experience than the first, in a good way.

After only about six hours of labor, Jeremy Adam was born, weighing 7 pounds, 2 ounces and we looked forward to our lives with him—holding him, blessing him, teaching him his ABC's, singing songs, and teaching him how to ride a bike.

Little did I know, however, that the pain I endured getting him into the world would be rivalled by the pain I would endure later, in my heart. Little did I know that the words, "It's a boy" introduced me to a spiritual and emotional dynamic that I hadn't begun and wouldn't ever begin with my daughter. Welcome to the world of sons and their moms.

Now you may also be a mother of a son through adoption, and you are in no way exempt from all the joy, sweetness, and sorrow of raising boys. Congratulations to you as well. You are blessed to be a mother. Here's what I know about you already: you have tolerated toilet humor at the dinner table more times than you want to admit, you have explained and demonstrated the amazing skill of *washing* your hands "with soap" a *million* times and you have shouted the phrase, "Get down from there!" more times than you can count. You may even have said the words, "I brought you into this world and I can take you out!" It's ok. You're not alone.

Here's what I also know about you: you are strong, and you are courageous. You are also giving. No one can be a mother without the incredible ability to deny oneself—to grit one's teeth and give, even when you feel like there is nothing more to give. You have tenacity and you are a fighter. Motherhood is not for wimps.

Unfortunately, after all the trials and challenges we go through with young boys and teenagers, there is still one more challenge we will have to face. In the likely event that your son meets a young woman with whom he wants to build a life, inevitably, you will have to overcome the sorrow and emotional pain of letting him go, even after you've invested so much into him. No mother of a son is immune to this natural and biblical occurrence. Initially, separation from mom will be slight and gradual as he identifies more with his father, but then as he gets older and prepares for *the other woman*, separation must become much more distinct and permanent.

During the first number of years of a child's life, the mother is first and primary as she meets all the needs of her child—feeding him and caring for him. Dad helps but is very much in the background. Mom very quickly bonds with the baby and continues to be the one the child is most attached to and drawn to—not wanting to be out of her presence and many times wanting to be held and attached at the hip, quite literally. However, by the second year, there begins to be a shift marking a difference between our relationships with sons and daughters.

Dr. James Dobson says in his book, *Bringing Up Boys*:

> "Girls continue to grow in their identification with their mothers. On the other hand, a boy has an additional developmental task – to disidentify from his mother and identify with his father. At this point (beginning about eighteen months), a little boy will not only begin to observe the difference, he must now decide, 'Which one am I going to be?' In making this shift in identity, the little boy begins to take his father as a model of masculinity." [1]

Even though a boy will shift at an early age to begin to identify with his father, hopefully looking up to and wanting to emulate him, boys still are *highly* emotionally connected to their mother as their mother is still the *primary* woman in their lives. The father doesn't replace the mother, but an important relationship with the father (or male role model) begins to be forged and a boy learns what it is to be a man.

---

[1] Dr. James Dobson, *Bringing Up Boys* (Carol Stream: Tyndale House, 2001), 120. Print.

The separation that will rip at your heart comes later. It comes when he decides to love another woman, other than you and put her first, as long as they both shall live. The deepest wound comes when you have the last dance with him at his wedding and you separate emotionally from your boy who has now grown into a man. Some women protest and think, "It doesn't have to be that way," but my friend, it does. In the upcoming chapters, we will delve deeper into why, as well as take a step back and look deep into how God made us, what our needs are, and why we as mothers struggle to let our sons go. In the second half of the book, we will discuss surviving and thriving after he's gone.

Come with me dear friend; take my hand. Let's journey through this difficult terrain together and navigate through our toughest challenge yet—you and me together, woman to woman. Let's be real and let's get honest about our hearts and rise, going from glory to glory. With Christ in us and by our side, we can do all things through Him who gives us strength and loves us unconditionally.

I pray this book encourages you, touches you and gives you the tools, ideas, strategies, and Godly revelation you need to move forward into a clear identity and abundant life filled with love and peace, in Christ.

Part I

Experiencing the Waves

Two Become One

Our oldest son Jeremy is now 22 years old. He's gradually preparing to move into a life on his own and grow his own little family apart from us. To say that this is not difficult to accept would be a downright lie. Frankly, it really stinks, because I know that he will get busy trying to meet all the obligations that come with a wife and family. All of me wants him to be outrageously successful and happy; most of me wants him to be super independent because then I know we did our job well, but a small part of me wants him to still need me, so I know he'll have a reason to call. I already miss him, and he still lives at home! Lord, help me.

I know that many reading this book are further along in this journey than I am. Just last week a good friend told me the emotional story about her last dance with her son at his wedding. Through tears, she explained to me how she felt the moment when the emotional disconnect happened between them, as they finished their dance and let go of each other's hands. She went back to her husband, and her son to his bride.

There was now a new woman who took first place in his heart and my friend had to fade off into the distance. It made me emotional just listening to her, knowing that one day I would be in those same shoes. She also briefly told me about the conversation she had with her son prior, talking about the separation that had to occur. Wow, I deeply respect this woman of God, facing this challenge head on, not running from it or trying to hang on for dear life, sharing her heart openly with her son so there was clarity in their minds—no misunderstandings or hurt feelings. They both were prepared, ready and clear on the expectations of the other—a beautiful position for love and respect to continue to thrive in their relationship.

Despite it feeling excruciatingly painful, this occurrence of leaving and separating from our sons is biblical and the more we can cooperate with it and prepare for it, the better.

Genesis 2:23-24 says the following:

> The man said, "This is now bone of my bones and flesh of my flesh; she shall be called 'woman,' for she was taken out of man." That is why a man leaves his father and mother and is united to his wife, and they become one flesh.

Did you notice the order of the last verse? It is very important. The man must leave his father and mother *first* and only then can he be united *as one* with his wife, properly, in spirit and in soul. If we don't let them leave emotionally, or if we don't remove ourselves, we become an obstacle to their lives together—possibly even becoming a hindrance to bearing the physical fruit of oneness.

A number of years ago I was at a house church with friends and as we were in worship, the Lord told me that a certain young man in the room was having trouble conceiving with his wife. As an intercessor, I get words of knowledge about people from time to time for the purpose of praying for them effectively (NIV calls it a "message of knowledge" in 1 Cor.12:8). So, I asked the Lord, "What do you want me to do about it?" and as I looked at the young man, I *saw* (internally in my spirit) an umbilical cord coming out from his abdomen. I knew as soon as I saw it, the Lord was showing me that he was still attached to his mother. The Lord reminded me of Genesis 2:24 so I shared it with him and explained the necessity of leaving his mother first to cleave to his wife properly. I then encouraged him to cut the umbilical cord. He took an actual pair of scissors and in a prophetic act, cut the cord. About eight weeks later, he announced on Facebook that he and his wife were expecting their first child.

This young man cut the cord that was in the spirit, but in his natural life, what did he need to do? Practically what did that mean? Did it mean he had to cut off relationship with his mom? Absolutely not! But it did mean he needed to draw some boundaries and it also meant he needed to stop letting his mother have so much influence over him as an adult and as a married man. He also had to emotionally separate from his mom which meant he had to stop looking to her as a *primary* source of love and emotional support—allowing his wife to now take that place.

Once a man marries, his wife must come first, after God of course, but before his mother. He must operate in the proper, Godly, *order of relationships*. We, as mothers, also need to do our part, butt out of what's not our business and stop trying to control him or have influence over their decisions. This is the time in your son's life for him to regulate and motivate himself, make his own decisions, and then live with the consequences, good or bad. It's time for him to be an adult and it's time for you to treat him as such.

Your success at transitioning in your relationship with your son actually began long before now—long before he even thought about marriage. Success begins by raising a son who has been taught and shown compassion for others and how to love others well. It begins with a healthy, loving connection of respect and honor for each other with proper boundaries in place from the start. Cultivating this takes work and diligence through years of growing. Loving your son well teaches him and enables him to love others well too.

The famous love passage from 1 Corinthians tells us clearly what love looks like:

> Love is patient, love is kind. It does not envy, it does not boast, it is not proud. It does not dishonor others, it is not self-seeking, it is not easily angered, it keeps no record of wrongs. Love does not delight in evil but rejoices with the truth. It always protects, always trusts, always hopes, always perseveres. Love never fails (1 Cor. 13:4-8a).

In light of this, we know that mothers and fathers were meant to love their children with all patience, understanding, kindness, humility, selflessness, honor, self-control, perseverance and forgiveness—never failing to provide a safe and secure place of belonging; protecting, disciplining and encouraging their children always; and wanting the best for them—all while drawing out of them courage and confidence as well as the gifts and abilities within. It's a lot to expect. Nonetheless, that is the job description.

I am no expert at parenting. That is for sure. In fact, even right now we are trying to navigate a difficult situation with one of our younger sons that just kind of erupted in the last few days. It threw me for a loop and had me questioning whether I should even be writing this book. Again, I am not an expert and I'm not trying to pretend that I know how to do this perfectly. I am just a momma with a gift for writing, a heart for others and an understanding of how to navigate emotional turmoil because of experience with and from the Lord.

If you have trained your son to think of others first and loved him well, it is time now for you to trust that what you've taught him will stick and that he will make good decisions based on his training. It is also time to trust in the Lord to do His part. It's not easy, but it is necessary. Proverbs 22:6 says, "Dedicate your children to God and point them in the way that they should go, and the values they've learned from you will be with them for life" (TPT).

There are no guarantees in life, so I know at this point it may feel scary. Just the thought of letting your son go may terrify you. Others may even feel *entitled* to maintain a close relationship, wanting him to call or text every day; after all, you've given him so much. Beloved, this is just not reasonable with an *adult* son. He has a life to live. Keeping in touch once a week is much more reasonable and will take the pressure off him. The last thing we want to do is make our adult son(s) feel smothered and controlled.

Beloved, if you are finding this difficult, keep pressing on and keep reading. There are a few things that can interfere with your ability to adjust, and we will address those things in the upcoming chapters. Remember God loves family just as much as you do and He wants us to maintain close, loving bonds that are appropriate, with each one of our adult children. He will lead you to what that looks like if you will surrender to His will and ask Him to teach you.

Relationship Over Religion

I'll never forget the day love ran deep like a rushing river, right into my heart. It was a gesture from our son Jeremy, I had never expected. It spoke volumes about his character and how he felt about me as his mother. We stood in line, one mother and son duo behind the other, at the edge of the football field.

It was a special game that day; they were raising funds for breast cancer research. All the young men were dressed in their regular game attire and protective gear—everything from their cleats to their helmets, except for one thing—the bright pink socks stretching to their knees. The bright pink socks though, were not the only thing that set this game apart from the rest. At this game, all the mothers were invited to enter the field with their player, as they were introduced at the beginning. It was such a privilege to be recognized and honored in this way.

As we stood there, waiting our turn, I noticed one duo entering the field holding hands and I immediately thought, "Oh that poor boy. He's probably so embarrassed holding his mother's hand." Never in a million years would I have expected this from my seventeen-year-old son, in public, on display in front of sixty of his peers, but our turn came and suddenly out of nowhere, Jeremy held out his hand and waited for me to take it. I was stunned. I looked at his hand, frozen for a second in disbelief. "Are you sure?" I asked him. He nodded. As I held back tears, heart pounding, I put my hand in his and we entered the field with our heads held high. The community watched and cheered us on. This was probably the proudest moment of my life. What a son! I will never forget it.

There have been several moments in my life when I have been completely overwhelmed with the goodness of God as I have seen my children shine. Jeremy has blown me away a few times with his compassion for others; he seems to have received an impartation of a powerful ability to love others well.

There was a day around Christmas when we saw a man begging for a handout in the parking lot of Walmart. I said to Jeremy, "Let's go get him some food." We drove across the street to Arby's and purchased a meal for him. I didn't expect Jeremy to help pay for it; he was only sixteen at the time, but he insisted.

This ability to love others well certainly doesn't come naturally for us, at least not in our fallen state, nor is it something that can necessarily just be taught. It can certainly be modelled, and my husband and I have tried our best, but I would have to give full credit to the Lord. Whatever we have done right has been because of the Lord's enabling; all we had to do was co-operate with Him. This ability to love well, is a grace that comes directly from God. It is a measure of God's heart that my son has apprehended, and it gives him a tremendous ability to empathize with others and to express love in tangible ways—even to the point of making sacrifices to do so.

Unfortunately, not too many of us are able to express *any* level of *sacrificial* love, nor do we receive it from anyone else. In fact, too many of us have felt like we have grown up in loveless homes or at least a home where love was surface and shallow at best. Maybe we heard the words, "I love you," but there was no action to follow it up—or perhaps the words, "I love you" were not even uttered and you wondered if you were loved at all.

My parents did the best they could with what they had. Most parents do. Unfortunately, very often it isn't enough, and we end up insecure, looking for love in all the wrong places. As an adult, the depth of the issue hit home to me the day of my maternal grandmother's funeral. With the Lord's help, I was able to work through my own issues, forgiving my parents and receiving love from God, but this day I saw with clarity how the lack of love in childhood affects us and carries on through the generations.

My grandmother had been 99 years old when she passed—just shy of her 100th birthday. After the funeral, I quickly exited through the back door to escape into the sunshine and warmth of the summer day, out of the dismal depressing atmosphere of the funeral home. My mother followed shortly after. I turned to look at her and she said with a pathetic childlike voice, "My mother never loved me." I was stunned by her statement.

I realized in that moment that aside from any intervention from the Lord and wisdom He may give us, we learn how to love others by how we were loved. I had never felt tremendously loved by my own mother and now she was confessing the same thing about hers. This was an "aha" moment for me; it is a cycle—a cycle with no end, unless someone sees it, makes the decision to do something about it and asks the Lord to intervene and teach them a better way— to give them a heart of love and empower them to move in a new way.

First John 4:8 tells us, "God is love." It's not that He's loving; it's more than that. His very character is love. He is the embodiment of love. Additionally, in Genesis 1:26 God says, "Let us make mankind in our image, in our likeness," then again in verse 27 it states, "So God created mankind in his own image, in the image of God he created them; male and female he created them." The original Hebrew word translated "image" in these verses, is *tselem* which actually has the connotation of a phantom or illusion. In other words, God designed us so much like Himself, it was almost illusionary. In fact, when the Lord looked at Adam and Eve, it was almost as if He was looking at Himself.[2] We were created in the image of love. We were made to look like love, made from love, for love and to love. In the beginning love was at our core.

Awe, the garden! It must have been such a tranquil place, so much peace and beauty, Adam and Eve in communion with God the Father, Jesus and the Holy Spirit, all in one place and all at One with each other. They strolled through the garden together in the cool of the day, enjoying each other's presence, and loving one another well—no shame, no fear and no lack. They were family as family was intended to be.

It's clear in Genesis though that in the garden, man had a job to do— it wasn't all just strolling and relaxing. God appointed man as the keeper of the garden (Gen.2:15), ruling over what He had created (Gen.1:26). Adam tended the garden faithfully, working the land, but the Garden of Eden was different than

---

[2] Dutch Sheets, *Intercessory Prayer* (Ventura: Regal Books, 1996), 26. Print.

any other garden that we are used to. This garden co-operated. This garden responded to Adam's work. There was no sweat on his brow; there was no toil and no hardship. The land yielded to Adam just as God designed it and Adam yielded to God, doing what he was designed to do.

The Garden of Eden was a paradise. Everyone's needs were met, in relationship with each other. Unfortunately, something happened to interrupt that paradise and harmony together. Temptation came in the form of a crafty snake whispering lies and sowing seeds of doubt and rejection into Eve's heart. A forbidden piece of fruit was picked, eaten and shared, causing rebellion to come to full bloom (Gen.3:1-6). As a result, man's perfect relationship with God ended abruptly. Instead of strolling with God through the garden, Adam and Eve hid from God out of shame and fear (Gen.3:7-8). Their relationship with God was broken, their communion severed as they were banished from their home. Their need for connection to their Maker and their need for His love was no longer being met. A gaping hole in their hearts yearned for what was lost.

Outside of the garden as orphans, they were now forced to become independent, doing their best to look after their own needs—toiling, sweating from their brow, working the land that was now resistant to bearing fruit. The land had become hard, full of weeds and briers, matching the state of their hearts. Hearts were broken, spirits and souls broken, longing to be back in relationship.

This is where we are today. The plight of Adam and Eve passed down from generation to generation, all the way to now. We think we're immune. We think we're over it, but we're not. The good news is that Father God misses us too and He didn't want to be separated from us either. He simply didn't have any other choice. Even as God is love, He is also just, and cannot turn a blind eye to sin. So, God came up with a genius plan that would satisfy both His love and His justice. He Himself, sent His Son Jesus Christ from Heaven down to earth, in the humble form of a baby. The Son of God came to take back the keys of the Kingdom, to destroy the works of the devil and to become a sin offering for us.

Even though the paradise of the garden was interrupted, we can accept His gift of salvation through faith in Christ Jesus and be restored back to the Father, becoming His beloved child once again. We can be in communion with our Heavenly Father again and be united back into His family. This is a supernatural occurrence we can enter once we have repented of our sins, believed on Jesus Christ, and turned the control of our lives over to Him. Indeed, we were created with a need for relationship and love and these needs can be fulfilled by God alone. We could even, if we so choose, live at peace in solitude with Christ—that is how strong the connection can and should be *felt*. If you don't live in that reality yet, don't worry, you will read more on how to get there in the upcoming chapters (if you haven't submitted your life to Christ yet, please skip right now, to appendix A at the back of the book (pg. 111) and work through what's there. Mark this page and come back here to meet me when you're done).

You may have heard the good news of Jesus Christ already and perhaps you are a Christian. Perhaps you go to church, believe the Word of God, and faithfully serve your community. That's amazing and that's a big first step in the right direction. Many people are doing this already. However, there is a step further that many don't know about and don't take to *experience* God and His amazing love.

If your Christian life is more about simply believing something and following a set of rules, you're missing out and probably still *feel* less than completely loved. This next step is a step into a real, living *relationship* with our living God through the Holy Spirit where you actually hear His voice and experience His power. Perhaps you've heard this before, "relationship over religion." It has been a theme in some Christian circles as of late, which is awesome, but I wonder what your thoughts are on it. At this point, all I ask is for you to hear me out and trust that just as the Lord has orchestrated this book to be in your hands, He is also orchestrating your deliverance from a dry and barren place, void of authentic true love and acceptance.

Beloved, the Lord has promised to give you good gifts when you ask, and I know you've asked! You've cried out, you've wept, and you've looked and waited for love. God is about to reveal himself to you in brand new ways and you are about to have your socks blessed right off!

Matthew 7:7-11 says the following:

> Ask, and the gift is yours. Seek, and you'll discover. Knock, and the door will be opened for you. For every persistent one will get what he asks for. Every persistent seeker will discover what he longs for. And everyone who knocks persistently will one day find an open door. 'Do you know of any parent who would give his hungry child, who asked for food, a plate of rocks instead? Or when asked for a piece of fish, what parent would offer his child a snake instead? If you, imperfect as you are, know how to lovingly take care of your children and give them what's best, how much more ready is your heavenly Father to give wonderful gifts to those who ask him? (TPT)

You can trust your Heavenly Father to lead you and guide you on this journey and to meet you where you are. He wants to have a real, intimate relationship with you, and He wants you to feel His love, experience His power and know His heart.

Stick with me, beloved as we continue exploring this territory together. Ask and expect the Lord to do a work in your heart, so you can know, beyond a shadow of a doubt, that you are loved without measure. Once you do, it will be so much easier to let go and trust God in this difficult time.

Fully Immersed in Him

Back in the early 80's I was obsessed with a song by Foreigner called, *I Wanna Know What Love Is*. You may know it, depending on your age. The chorus goes like this: "I wanna know what love is, I want you to show me; I wanna feel what love is, I know you can show me." Sing it with me ladies! Was this one of your favorites too? As I swayed to the music at fifteen years old, I was crying out to whomever... anyone! I just wanted to *feel* loved by someone.

One day, I played that song on repeat in my bedroom for an hour until finally my father burst into my room and exclaimed, "Don't you know that God loves you?" It was a good question! I had been to Sunday school almost all fifteen years of my young life, but everything I knew about God I only knew in my head. I had given mental assent to everything I had been taught, but my heart was not penetrated by the love of God.

My siblings and I had grown up in a church that was *not* a mainline Christian denomination. Regardless, we were taught well on who the Father is. We were taught that God is good, that He is faithful, ever-present, and all-powerful—that He is love and loves us unconditionally, but I really struggled to believe in the love of God for *me*. I needed more than words, head knowledge and unfulfilled promises.

I believe the reason why my heart was not touched by the love of God, is because we weren't taught the *full* truth about who Jesus is (God made flesh, Col. 1:15-17, John 1:1-14) and why He was crucified—after all He is the Way, the Truth and the Life and no one comes to the Father except through Him (John 14:6). The truth about Jesus and His incredible sacrifice for me was missing. The voice of the Father was a faint, faint, whisper that I could barely hear until… at the age of 22, my Way Maker, Jesus Christ, stepped into His intercessory role, between me and the Father ushering in the Holy Spirit to flood me with His grace and power; only then did the Lord's voice become loud and clear. We all lined up according to the Father's plan: me, the Holy Spirit, Jesus, and finally the Father, giving me access to His voice.

Finally, the truth was made plain, and it all made sense. My confusion and unbelief a thing of the past. I thank God for the encounter with my sister when she told me who Jesus really is and all the pain and suffering He endured, was to purchase me back and re-unite me with our heavenly Father—all because of His great love, *for me*. For God so loved ME, that He sent His One and only Son. This blew my mind! This was the first time to my knowledge that someone had sacrificed anything for me. This one ACT of love touched me deeply. Jesus wasn't and isn't just a man of empty words; He is THE Word; He keeps His Word, and He ACTS on it. He is trustworthy.

God's love for us has been made crystal clear through His sacrifice for us and when we get a revelation of the depth of this love, it causes us to love Him in return. True love for God, however, is active. It's not passive. Christ said in John 14:21:

> Whoever has my commands and keeps them is the one who loves me. The one who loves me will be loved by my Father, and I too will love them and show myself to them.

Loving God looks like having a heart that wants to please Him, praise Him and be holy. Keeping God's commands is an outward working of our love relationship with Him and becomes possible with the Holy Spirit living in us, empowering us to do what we can't on our own.

In addition to our inward heart attitude is our outward expressions of love for God. This may look different for everyone, but one beautiful example is found in Luke 7:36-47. Jesus has a glorious encounter with a woman in the home of a Pharisee that goes like this:

> When one of the Pharisees invited Jesus to have dinner with him, he went to the Pharisee's house and reclined at the table. A woman in that town who lived a sinful life learned that Jesus was eating at the Pharisee's house, so she came there with an alabaster jar of perfume. As she stood behind him at his feet weeping, she began to wet his feet with her tears. Then she wiped them with her hair, kissed them and poured perfume on them. When the Pharisee who had invited him saw this, he said to himself, "If this man were a prophet, he would know who is touching him and what kind of woman she is—that she is a sinner." Jesus answered him, "Simon, I have something to tell you." "Tell me teacher," he said. "Two people owed money

to a certain moneylender. One owed him five hundred denarii, and the other fifty. Neither of them had the money to pay him back, so he forgave the debts of both. Now which of them will love him more?" Simon replied, "I suppose the one who had the bigger debt forgiven." "You have judged correctly," Jesus said. Then he turned toward the woman and said to Simon, "Do you see this woman? I came into your house. You did not give me any water for my feet, but she wet my feet with her tears and wiped them with her hair. You did not give me a kiss, but this woman, from the time I entered, has not stopped kissing my feet. You did not put oil on my head, but she has poured perfume on my feet. Therefore, I tell you, her many sins have been forgiven—as her great love has shown. But whoever has been forgiven little loves little." (Luke 7:36-47)

This story reminds me of Matthew 19:23 that says it's hard for the rich to enter the kingdom of heaven. The Pharisee was rich in knowledge, rich in wisdom and resources; he thought he had everything he needed. When we are rich, whether it be in resources or spirit, we don't see our need and we're not grateful for the Lord's sacrifice. I love the sinful woman's humility as she poured out her love on Jesus. She loved Him well in response to His great love for her. It was easy for her because she knew she had been forgiven so much.

The Lord's great demonstration of love also met *my* great need, making it easy for me to fall head over heels in love with Him. Jesus and I began our wild love affair in January of 1989, and I never looked back; my love and passion for Him grew continuously (with ebbs and flows of course) and still does. Now, I am conscience of His presence with me always. We speak with one another at will and we are also comfortable in our silence together; I can't live without Him. His love is like a continuous river flowing into my soul. When I take time to be still and sit to enjoy Him, that river becomes like a rushing river that can't be stopped. Jesus gave me everything. Now I am honored to give Him everything back in return—my life, time, children, family, gifts, talents, abilities, and resources. He is worthy!

What about you, beloved? What is Jesus worth to you? Is He worth a passionate pursuit? Is He worth getting excited about? Unfortunately, so many Christians are stuck, and they don't even realize it. Here are some good questions to help you evaluate: Honestly speaking, how much of yourself and your life have you *surrendered* to Him? ALL or just a portion? Do you segregate your life, giving Jesus just Sundays? Do you attempt to connect with Jesus through the week with quiet times, devotions, Bible reading and prayer? Do you give Him 15 minutes a day or do you give Him every minute, of every day?

If you're thinking, "Whoa, that's a lot to ask!" or "How can I possibly do that? I've got stuff to do!" Let me explain. I'm not suggesting you lock yourself up in a closet and just read your Bible and pray all day. Clearly that's not doable and it's not necessary. The Lord does not want us getting all bound up in spiritual rituals and routines. What I'm suggesting is to *practice His presence*—become aware of His presence with you all the time. That way you don't forget about Him and go for days without communing with Him and you can pray whisper prayers to Him throughout your day as needed and led by the Holy Spirit.

How do we become aware of His presence? We ask Jesus to baptize, or fully immerse us in the supernatural power of the Holy Spirit. It's not about trying harder or carving out more quiet time with Him; it's ALL about baptism according to the scriptures and exercising our senses to discern His presence and hearing His voice. When this happens, we become God-conscience, and we can let go of being self-conscience.

Numerous times in the Bible we are told that the Lord will never leave us or forsake us. In other words, He is with us ALL the time. That's His promise. He is with us during our quiet times, and He is with us when we go about our day doing our chores and driving our *taxis*, dropping kids off here and there, doing laundry, washing dishes, working out, and even when scrolling Facebook. The Holy Spirit connects us to His presence and will give us an awareness of Him, so we are free to have a continual conversation in our hearts, lifting our praise and our concerns 24/7.

We don't have to be sitting in a certain chair to pray and we don't even have to have our eyes closed to pray. We can pray anytime, anywhere. I'm not knocking the beautiful practice of concentrated prayer time in a special place. I'm simply suggesting that we can pray in addition to that time, all day, in whatever we are doing.

After Jesus' resurrection and ascension, He sent the Holy Spirit to be with us, to comfort us, to be our advocate and helper. Now, the Holy Spirit is our connection to heaven. Jesus says in the following verses that it's the Holy Spirit who speaks to us, He (Jesus) will speak to us *through* the Holy Spirit, and He will tell us what is to come.

> But very truly I tell you, it is for your good that I am going away. Unless I go away, the Advocate will not come to you; but if I go, I will send him to you. When he comes, he will prove the world to be in the wrong about sin and righteousness and judgement: (John 16:7-8)

> "I have much more to say to you, more than you can now bear. But when he, the Spirit of truth, comes, he will guide you into all the truth. He will not speak on his own; he will speak only what he hears, and he will tell you what is yet to come. He will glorify me because

it is from me that he will receive what he will make known to you. (John 16:12-14)

Robert Boyd Munger has written a very well-known devotional booklet called, *My Heart – Christ's Home.* You may have heard of it. This devotional introduces readers to what it means to surrender every aspect of their lives to the control of Christ by using an analogy of rooms in our home. I've actually not read it in its entirety, but I love the idea. Using this same analogy, imagine that salvation (repenting, believing, confessing, and surrendering) is like inviting Christ in through the front door. The front door is the entrance, and the Lord has come in. He has brought life and light back into our home, but where does He reside? Does He just stay in the foyer or is He welcomed into *every* room? Is He restricted to the formal living room where things are in order or is He free to roam, to open closets and cupboards and look under the bed? Is He treated like a guest or like He belongs there? Is He treated like part of the family or is He treated properly—like He is the head of the family?

Perhaps Jesus is honored well, given access to every room, and received as the authority figure in the home, but what about the Holy Spirit? The Holy Spirit is not synonymous with Jesus; they are not the same, but two separate members of the Godhead with different assignments and roles in our lives. Do we invite the Holy Spirit in and honor Him the same way we honor Christ?

Here's what I fear happens in denominations that don't believe in the *baptism* of the Holy Spirit: we open the door, and the Holy Spirit comes in, but then we immediately stuff Him into the front hall closet, not permitting Him to move, fill the house nor do any of what He desires to do, such as heal, comfort, transform and communicate truth.

Unfortunately, some Christians don't trust the supernatural demonstrations of God through the Holy Spirit as it can feel strange, and we can't understand it with our natural mind. It can offend our flesh, but we must allow our mind and our experience to be governed by the Spirit, not the flesh. Romans 8:6-8 says the following:

> The mind governed by the flesh is death, but the mind governed by the Spirit is life and peace. The mind governed by the flesh is hostile to God; it does not submit to God's law, nor can it do so. Those who are in the realm of the flesh cannot please God.

Friends, to experience the supernatural love of God, we are going to have to be willing to experience His supernatural Spirit. We should not be afraid to let the Holy Spirit do what He wants to do. He wants to bless us outrageously and heal us on the inside. I have had some of the most profound, amazing healing experiences flat on my back, on the floor, completely overtaken by the power of God, as the Holy Spirit ministered to me through visions on the screen of my imagination. He has taken me back to some very painful and traumatic experiences and brought me through them again amidst His presence, completely changing my memory of them. The only reason it was possible for God to do this for me was because I was willing to submit to Him. I was willing to give Holy Spirit control. I've said it already, but I will say it again: God does not trump our own free will and He will not do what you do not want Him to do; it is very possible to resist the Holy Spirit and His work in you.

Many people ask, "Why would God do that? Why would God cause someone to shake, fall to their knees, weep or fall to the floor?" First, I would say that God's goal is not for us to be on the floor. His goal is to heal us and bless us, but when the supernatural power of God begins to move on us and we surrender, our flesh is going to react. No one can see God in His *full* Glory and live (Ex. 33:20), so why are we surprised when we get a *small glimpse* of His Glory, and we can't stand or maintain our composure? Our flesh is temporal, in the natural realm and must be trained by exposure to be able to stand under the Glory—this is why people in the Bible fell down when the Lord manifested himself to them. One example of this is Saul on the road to Damascus, at his conversion (see Acts 9:4). This is also why Moses' countenance shone after spending time in the Glory (Ex.34:29-35).

Ephesians 3:16-19 tells us that we are strengthened and empowered *through the Holy Spirit* to grasp the love of God for us and when we do, we will be filled to the measure of the fullness of God. I, therefore, encourage you right now to position yourself to receive the Holy Spirit's empowering and strength through baptism in the Holy Spirit.

John the Baptist says in Matthew 3:11:

> "I baptize you with water for repentance. But after me comes one who is more powerful than I, whose sandals I am not worthy to carry. He will baptize you with the Holy Spirit and fire.

Much like baptism in water completely *submerges* us in Jesus and is a separate experience from believing the Good News, baptism in the Holy Spirit also completely *submerges* us in Him and is a separate experience from being born again. The experience of believing and the experience of being baptized in the Holy Spirit can be easily understood by comparing the act of drinking a glass of water to the act of diving into a pool.

When we believe the Good News, we drink of the Holy Spirit, and He causes our spirits to come alive as He takes up residence within us. When we ask Jesus to *baptize* us in the Holy Spirit, it's like diving into the Holy Spirit just as we would a pool, allowing ourselves to be completely overtaken, saturated in Him, inside and out. The Holy Spirit comes *in* us and *on* us completely.

Acts 8:14-17 records one example of the baptism of the Holy Spirit being a separate event from believing and being baptized in water. It reads the following:

> When the apostles in Jerusalem heard that Samaria had accepted the word of God, they sent Peter and John to Samaria. When they arrived, they prayed for the new believers there that they might receive the Holy Spirit, because the Holy Spirit had not yet come on any of them; they had simply been baptized in the name of the Lord Jesus. Then Peter and John placed their hands on them, and they received the Holy Spirit.

Lastly, the disciples themselves had two different experiences receiving the Holy Spirit. The first time was when Jesus first appeared to the disciples in the upper room after His resurrection. Jesus said to them in John 20:21-22, "Peace be with you! As the Father has sent me, I am sending you. And with that he breathed on them and said, 'Receive the Holy Spirit.'"

Later, on a different occasion before Jesus ascended, while they ate a meal together, Jesus instructed His disciples to stay in Jerusalem until they were "baptized with the Holy Spirit" because then they would receive the power necessary to continue on in the ministry.

> On one occasion, while he was eating with them, he gave them this command: "Do not leave Jerusalem, but wait for the gift my Father promised, which you have heard me speak about. For John baptized with water, but in a few days you will be baptized with the Holy Spirit" (Acts 1:4-5).

This second experience that Jesus spoke about happened at Pentecost. They had waited in the upper room as per Jesus' instructions and the Holy Spirit sovereignly came on them and clothed them in His power, causing them to witness to the crowds of people gathered in Jerusalem for the feast, speaking to them in foreign languages they did not naturally know. This was the first manifestation of the power of God on the disciples. Two experiences for the disciples and two for us (for more on this topic, see John Bevere's book, *The Holy Spirit*).

Have I gotten off on a tangent here? Have I gone down a bunny trail? No. Beloved, the first steps in your ability to adjust and cope with your son leaving the family is to be able to discern the Lord's presence with you, to be secure in the love of God, and to be able to receive the love of God through the Holy Spirit so it makes a difference in your life. *In God's arms is the most Godly and honorable place for us to have our love needs met.*

Have you ever looked for love in all the wrong places? I have. When I was young, it was boyfriends. When I got older it was shopping, food, and friends. If we don't get our needs met in Christ we could end up in sin and worse yet, putting a heavy burden on our children by trying to get it from them.

As we wrap up this chapter, I would encourage you to spend some quiet time with the Lord. Pray how you are led, ask the Lord if there is anything you need to confess and turn away from, then honestly tell Him, "Lord Jesus, I'm ready. I'm ready to receive the Holy Spirit in His fullness." Ask Him, "Lord Jesus, would you baptize me in the Holy Spirit? Would you cause me to be completely submerged in Him? I want to experience all of you Lord, and I submit myself to you and your will. Holy Spirit come and fill me and overtake me; I give you permission to change me, heal me and transform me, from the inside out. Help me to discern your love and hear your voice. In Jesus' Name, Amen."

Just as a final exercise, would you go to that story in Luke 7:36-47 about the woman pouring perfume on Jesus' feet? Read it slowly and thoughtfully out loud. Meditate on it. See the people. Hear the conversations and see their faces. Smell the perfume. Let the Holy Spirit speak to you and perhaps show you where *you* might be if *you* were in the story and why. Are you on the floor next to the woman, emulating her actions? Are you one of the sceptics, criticizing her, judging her? Are you a bystander? If so, what are you thinking? You may want to journal your experience and anything the Lord tells you or shows you. When you're done, let's continue together.

A Road to Wholeness

As we embark on this journey together, there are two questions we must consider: Where are we coming from and where are we going? These questions are important as they help to shine light on the road in between. The place we have come from has shaped who we are today and hopefully we are aware that we are not yet who we were fully intended to be nor are we finished our assignment on the earth. Indeed, we are both a masterpiece, completely loved by God and a work in progress simultaneously. God loves us perfectly, exactly where we are, but loves us enough not to let us stay there.

After we give our hearts to Christ, God invites us on a journey of spiritual formation, becoming more and more like His Son, Jesus. This journey is one of healing, letting go of who we are not and becoming who we truly are. Some Christians don't even realize it; they think they're done. They've made the decision to accept Christ and now they just wait until they can enter their heavenly home, but there is more, beloved, so much more! There is very much an opportunity before all of us to grow, to become better, to let go of the past, undo the damage done and become the full intentions of God's heart when He thought of us, designed us and ordained every day of our lives. I like to think of it as a process of sanctification where we become holy and set apart for Kingdom purposes.

While it's true, Christ makes ALL things new, some things are made new immediately and other things are made new over time, as you submit to God. I believe it depends on the revelation and encounter you have with Christ. When Saul encountered Christ on the road to Damascus, he was totally and completely changed as the manifest presence and Glory of God overtook him. Acts 9:3-9 says the following:

> As he neared Damascus on his journey, suddenly a light from heaven flashed around him. He fell to the ground and heard a voice say to him, "Saul, Saul, why do you persecute me?" "Who are you, Lord?" Saul asked. "I am Jesus, whom you are persecuting," he replied. "Now get up and go into the city, and you will be told what you must do." The men traveling with Saul stood there speechless; they heard the sound but did not see anyone. Saul got up from the ground, but when he opened his eyes he could see nothing. So they led him by the hand into Damascus. For three days he was blind, and did not eat or drink anything.

After this encounter, the Lord sent Ananias to pray for Saul's eyes and to restore his sight. Saul, later called Paul, was completely made new, even receiving new eyesight, changing his perspective on everything. There are others too that have had powerful encounters with God to the point of seeing His manifest presence, though most of us have not and revelation of Jesus comes gradually.

We are positionally sanctified completely before God immediately upon accepting Christ. God sees us as holy, but parts of our souls and bodies are not *immediately* transformed. Some behaviors and beliefs just fall away, but more often than not, we struggle with weaknesses in our flesh and sin patterns that have become habits. Our hearts yearn to be holy, but we don't walk it out perfectly. Perhaps we are like Paul when he wrote:

> For in my inner being I delight in God's law; but I see another law at work in me, waging war against the law of my mind and making me a prisoner of the law of sin at work within me. What a wretched man I am! Who will rescue me from this body that is subject to death? Thanks be to God, who delivers me through Jesus Christ our Lord! So then, I myself in my mind am a slave to God's law, but in my sinful nature a slave to the law of sin. (Romans 7:22-25)

The answer though is in the declaration immediately following in Romans 8:

> Therefore, there is now no condemnation for those who are in Christ Jesus, because through Christ Jesus the law of the Spirit who gives life has set you free from the law of sin and death. (Romans 8:1-2)

Indeed, even though in our flesh we struggle, there is no condemnation, and the power of sin and death no longer have any hold on us. Despite how it may feel or how strong the temptation is, in the power of the Holy Spirit, we do have the freedom to say no to sin; it's really just a matter of believing it and exercising that choice. Thankfully though, we can go boldly before the throne of God and receive forgiveness at any time. Hebrews 4:16 says:

So let us come boldly to the throne of our gracious God. There we will receive his mercy, and we will find grace to help us when we need it most. (NLT)

And first John 1:9 says, "If we confess our sins, he is faithful and just and will forgive us our sins and purify us from all unrighteousness."

As we navigate the waves of releasing our son to a wife, there is naturally going to be some emotions that arise; we may feel sad as we miss him, perhaps angry as we feel we are being replaced and he doesn't need us anymore, or lonely as we adjust and get used to him being gone. We may also be a bit nervous or fearful for him, "Is he going to make good decisions? Will he be successful?" This type of response is reasonable, however, despite that, some women will have an *exaggerated* response that sends them reeling into despair. It's possible for our lives and emotions to be turned completely upside down, for us to refuse to let go, holding on for dear life and desperately trying to maintain control of him.

Some crucial questions to ask ourselves are: Where am I in all of this? Am I thriving or just barely surviving? What is the degree of emotional upset within? How is my current response working for me and others? Am I adjusting or am I refusing to co-operate with the process? Am I loving well and being Godly amidst it all? Am I allowing my son to live his life or am I smothering him?

Before reading further there are two enemies you will need to put under your feet; they both cause us to stay stagnant and stuck where we are, not wanting to change or grow. Those enemies are pride and complacency. Without first recognizing these two things as enemies and overcoming them, it will be almost impossible to apply anything in this book. Decide right now, to be open and teachable, and believe in humility that we all need improvement, even you. Not one of us has arrived yet.

Complacency in this context could be described as a smug satisfaction with oneself and one's achievements accompanied by a lack of awareness or lack of willingness to recognize one's weaknesses or shortcomings. I don't know whether you've ever noticed, but sometimes even when what we are doing is NOT working for us, we continue to keep doing it the same old way—usually because we are convinced that we are right. We can also be convinced that it's easier to remain in what's familiar. "It may not be great, but at least I know what to expect. Where I am is tough, but I'm coping." Ever said or thought either of those statements?

Don't dig your heels in here friend; there is a better way. We are not supposed to be just surviving or coping. In Christ, we are supposed to be *thriving*. We can grow and we can heal if necessary. We can submit to God, allow Him to change us and enjoy more peace for doing it. We can come to a place of rest and holiness in Christ, within our own hearts, in our relationships and with our children.

Beloved, if you are amidst this trial now, something is coming to an end for you, but something else is also beginning. You are in a period of transition—saying goodbye to one way of doing things in your role as mother and entering another. It's always good to have an idea of how to navigate the change and perhaps what new thing is around the corner, but sometimes we don't see it coming nor what to expect. Sometimes we just need to trust that God has good plans for us and keep moving, one step at a time. As we go, moving forward healed and whole is vital and will help us to be successful in every season and assignment of our lives.

For the remainder of this book, we will take a journey to the healing of our emotions and hearts. I would encourage you to take small bites at a time in order to fully process what the Lord reveals. It might not be an easy journey, but walking this way will enable us to survive, thrive, love well and honor God as we are meant to.

Take heart beloved, your Savior Jesus has overcome the world and has already overcome each obstacle on your behalf. We need only to apply and appropriate His victory in our lives through repentance and confession. Let's experience the freedom of wholeness together.

Part II

Surviving & Thriving

From Orphan to Daughter

In chapter 2, we briefly talked about the Garden of Eden and the paradise that Adam and Eve enjoyed, being in perfect fellowship and harmony with God as their Father. We also talked about their fall to temptation and their disobedience—eating fruit from the tree of the knowledge of good and evil. The results of their transgression were deep and would be carried through the generations all the way down the line, to us. Genesis 3:17b–24 reads:

> "Cursed is the ground because of you; through painful toil you will eat food from it all the days of your life. It will produce thorns and thistles for you, and you will eat the plants of the field. By the sweat of your brow you will eat your food until you return to the ground, since from it you were taken; for dust you are and to dust you will return." Adam named his wife Eve, because she would become the mother of all the living.

> The Lord God made garments of skin for Adam and his wife and clothed them. And the Lord God said, "The man has now become like one of us, knowing good and evil. He must not be allowed to reach out his hand and take also from the tree of life and eat, and live forever." So the Lord God banished him from the Garden of Eden to work the ground from which he had been taken. After he drove the man out, he placed on the east side of the Garden of Eden cherubim and a flaming sword flashing back and forth to guard the way to the tree of life.

Adam and Eve were *banished* from the Garden and *separated* from their Father and their family. They became *orphans*, on the outside looking in, no longer welcome. They were forced to become independent looking after themselves, toiling and sweating to work the ground to grow their own food. *We* must do the same now.

Father God sent His Son Jesus to restore us back to Him and back to the way it was before the fall, but I wonder, even after we've accepted Christ, do we continue to live in a *pattern* or mindset of an orphan? Do we continue, despite God's promises, to insist on being independent from God doing our own thing and relying on ourselves?

Our spirits have come alive and the Holy Spirit lives in us and clothes us in His power. Our spirits are at one with God's Spirit, that is true, but are we able to walk in the cool of the day, in the garden with Him again? Are we able to experience God's presence to the extent of trusting Him fully? Do we trust Him to meet all our needs according to the riches of His Glory in Christ Jesus? What does that look like in everyday life? Have we stopped toiling and working to meet our own needs?

Hmm... Does that last question have you squirming? Am I suggesting that we all need to stop working to trust God? No, definitely not! Work is good—even Adam worked. But *why* do we work? What is our motivation? Do we work out of fear, or do we work because God has told us to? Is our work a step into our destiny and purpose with Him or are we desperately working any job we can get to pay the bills? Paying the bills is good, but are we in God's plan to pay the bills or our own?

I have waffled back and forth for years as to whether to get a part time job—trading time for money again, and the answer I receive from the Holy Spirit is always *no*. I would like to get a paycheck I can count on. It would be easier. However, that's not what God has called me to right now, so I continue to follow the voice of my good Shepherd going about my *Father's* business until He shows me something different. We all need to seek the Lord and follow where He leads. Some are anointed and called to work in the marketplace, and some are not.

How does an orphan live? An orphan lives *independently* and relies on oneself. They struggle for what they need, and they earn everything by the sweat of their brow. They work like dogs and *strive* to be accepted. They hoard and save things because they don't know when they will need that thing they never use. They eat fast fearing they won't get enough, and they stash food in their pockets for later, just in case. They are jealous of others, lack peace, lack a sense of security and belonging and they don't feel loved. Orphans don't feel protected, they don't trust, fears plague their mind, and they desperately search for safety in things and human relationships going from one person to the next.

Is it possible to be *saved* and know God, but still struggle with patterns of orphan living in your soul—to not live like a full son or daughter of God? Yes, it is. It takes healing, a paradigm shift in our thinking, a de-programming and renewing of the mind to really be able to believe and grasp the truth that God is a good and perfect Father that has promised to meet our needs. We don't even know what that is or what that looks like. None of us has ever had one before as none exist on this earth. Our earthly fathers, even the great ones, have all fallen short of the Glory of God somehow.

What holds us back from being a true daughter? What holds us in a pattern of orphan living? Perhaps it's the cutthroat way of the world that teaches us distorted messages: we must earn everything; nothing is just handed to us on a silver platter; look after number one; the only person we can rely on is ourselves; and if you want it done right, do it yourself. It also can be the negative experiences of our past creating negative expectations within us—expectations of hardship, not being looked after, neglected, rejected, and disappointed.

There were many things that happened in my young life that colored the way I saw myself. Over the years as a youngster, I had received many different messages that were in direct opposition to the truth—messages that told me I was unloveable, not good enough, not pretty enough, not wanted and not worth anyone's time. Healing from these messages had to come before I could see myself through my Heavenly Father's eyes and embrace my identity as a full daughter of God.

Shortly after our first child was born in 1994, I began to have some emotional upset I couldn't explain so I talked with a good friend who was a prayer counsellor. We met at her home and not long after we sat down to pray, I had a memory bubble up from my sub-conscience I had forgotten about.

I was little and secretly sitting in the hallway, listening to my mother on the telephone. She was having a private conversation with my grandmother and my young ears were where they should not have been, hearing things I should not have heard. Mom was frustrated and annoyed; I had done something to upset her, and she sent me to my room. Unbeknownst to her, I had snuck down the hallway and planted myself within ear shot. Mom's words cut deep and left scars for a long time. In her defense, she didn't know I was there, and she was so tired. Three children under three years old were taking a toll on her and my father was not much help at all.

I relayed the memory to my friend, and she began to pray, leading me into healing. The grace, power and compassion of God came in like a flood and suddenly a vision began to play on the screen of my imagination:

> I was a little girl amidst a crowd of other children, waiting for the arrival of a special guest who was coming to greet us and bless us. There was a barricade that kept us back, but there wasn't enough room for everyone in the front where we were sure to be greeted.
>
> It was crowded—five, six children deep, all pushing and vying for a position where they could receive. Not surprisingly, I was at the back not able to make my way closer, feeling disappointed and rejected. We all waited as the excitement grew and voices got louder. *He won't greet me; He probably won't even notice me*, I thought, as I passively allowed the others to push and jostle me back.
>
> Suddenly, there He was. He had arrived! He began coming down the line greeting and smiling at the children in the front. I watched Him, longing to be included, as He continued. Again, *He won't greet me*, I thought. *He won't even notice me*, but suddenly… everything changed.
>
> In the blink of an eye, supernaturally, my position changed, and I found myself right smack dab in the front row—no longer hidden. Right before me stood Jesus clothed in vibrant white, taking my hands in His,

gazing intently into my eyes. I became lost in His gaze and everyone else disappeared. His fiery blue eyes piercing right into mine—right into my soul, cutting away the lies and eradicating everything warring against the truth.

"Barbara, I love you," He said. Time slowed and His words hung in the air with fresh breath and new life. Once again, slower this time, "B-a-r-b-a-r-a, I love you." A few moments passed as I tried to take it all in. His eyes locked on mine, communicating past human limitations. As love overtook me, eyes wet with salty tears, I thought astonished... *He said my name. He just said my name. I never told Him my name. How does He know my name?* Over the next few moments, truth enlightened my heart. He greeted me. He knows me. He loves me. He wants me. I am His.

This was everything I needed. One encounter with Jesus and the Word transformed me from the inside out. Forgiveness flowed and healing came. What a Savior! What a friend.

There's a verse in the Bible, found in 2 Corinthians 3:18, that talks about beholding God's Glory—looking intently on Him and His character and admiring and loving what we see. When we *behold* someone, it means that what we see grabs our attention and we linger there, admiring what we see and noticing the details—in awe.

One day I was praying and enjoying intimacy with God, and I realized that as I looked intently upon God and beheld His Glory, He was also beholding me in return. I was immediately uncomfortable and looked away. God gently touched my face and turned it back to Himself, "Let me behold you" was His Word to me. Uhg! That was difficult. That was *really* hard. What about you? Would you allow Him to linger and look at you intently, studying your face, seeing all your imperfections all at once?

Trusting God and overcoming insecurities about our acceptance and worth is a challenge for most of us if we're honest. We must resist the temptation to look away. As we look into His eyes, the Lord will bring healing to our soul. Let's allow Him to love us and accept us just as we are.

One of my favorite accounts of healing in the Bible is the healing of the woman with the issue of blood found in Mark 5:24-34. She had been bleeding for twelve straight years! Can you imagine how tired she must have been? She had no ultra-thin *Always* sanitary napkins or tampons to use—not even those thick bulky pads my mother used. Nothing! Or perhaps just strips of cloth that had to be washed out by hand.

This poor woman had spent all the money she had on doctors, and no one could help her. She was desperate, an outcast and extremely sick. Jesus was her only hope and she knew it. She knew the power that Jesus carried, and she knew that if she could only touch His garments, she would be healed (Mark 5:28). This *unclean* woman was not allowed to be out in public, but she went anyway, even amid a crowd. She was determined. She would get her healing no matter what the cost. She faced her fear, pressed through obstacles, and crossed many social and religious boundaries, came up behind Jesus so she wouldn't be seen, and grabbed her miracle by faith.

> At once Jesus realized that power had gone out of him. He turned around in the crowd and asked, "Who touched my clothes?" "You see the people crowding against you," his disciples answered, "and yet you can ask, 'Who touched me?'" But Jesus kept looking around to see who had done it. Then the woman, knowing what had happened to her, came and fell at

his feet and, trembling with fear, told him the whole truth. He said to her, "Daughter, your faith has healed you. Go in peace and be freed from your suffering." (Mark 5:30-34)

She trembled with fear, but did you catch that last part? "Daughter." Amid the crowd, in front of all the people that had abandoned and rejected her for so long—Jesus calls her His daughter. This was the one thing she didn't expect. She thought she had to sneak up on Him, but Jesus received her, validated her, loved her, and confirmed to her that she was part of His family.

This is the acceptance and belonging that we all long for, isn't it? Some of us had that longing met by our earthly parents and some did not. Just like the *unclean* woman in the Bible, many of *us* have also been suffering with an issue of blood, but for us it has been a bleeding of the heart. Today, the Lord calls you His daughter as well. Today the Lord heals you, redeems you and calls you His own. How deeply do you need Him? Tell Him and He will meet you.

Here's the Word of God for you:

> But now, this is what the Lord says—he who created you, Jacob, he who formed you, Israel: "Do not fear, for I have redeemed you; I have summoned you by name; you are mine. (Isaiah 43:1)

Now, read it again, but this time put *your* name in place of Jacob and Israel.

> But now, this is what the Lord says—he who created you, _____ he who formed you, _____: "Do not fear, for I have redeemed you; I have summoned you by name; you are mine.

I love the next verse as well:

> When you pass through the deep, stormy sea, you can count on me to be there with you. When you pass through raging rivers, you will not drown. When you walk through persecution like fiery flames, you will not be burned; the flames will not harm you. (Isaiah 43:2, TPT)

> So in Christ Jesus you are all children of God through faith, for all of you who were baptized into Christ have clothed yourselves with Christ. There is neither Jew nor Gentile, neither slave nor free, nor is there male and female, for you are all one in Christ Jesus. If you belong to Christ, then you are Abraham's seed, and heirs according to the promise. (Galatians 3:26-29)

One big happy family!

Lastly, another great example of the Father's acceptance of us is the story of the prodigal son, in Luke 15:11-32. The story paraphrased goes something like this:

The youngest son severely insults his father and severs ties with his family by making a demand for his inheritance early. He basically says to his father, "You are dead to me." The son then leaves the family to go out on his own, squandering his money on wild living.

Eventually, he runs out of money, lives with the pigs for a time and finally when he has nothing to eat, he decides to swallow his pride and go home. He plans on asking his father for forgiveness so that maybe he will take him in as a hired hand—at least then he would have food to eat.

The son begins his journey home and even while he is still a long way off, his father who has been watching for him, sees him in the distance. His dignified Jewish father ditches his dignity, pulling his tunic up over his knees and *runs* to meet his son. No hesitation. The son says to his father, "Father; I have sinned against heaven and against you. I am no longer worthy to be called your son" (Luke 15:21), and here's the part I want to emphasize: his father's reaction is not of anger, rejection or disappointment, but of excitement, love and forgiveness.

> "But the father said to his servants, 'Quick! Bring the best robe and put it on him. Put a ring on his finger and sandals on his feet. Bring the fattened calf and kill it. Let's have a feast and celebrate. For this son of mine was dead and is alive again; he was lost and is found.' So they began to celebrate. (Luke 15:22-24)

Wow, what a reception! It didn't go at all like the son had expected; he expected to be part of the help, but instead he was totally restored to the family with all the benefits of a son. The son happily received everything his Father gave him, with no resistance or false pride. No need to prove himself or earn anything back. There was no probation period and no consequences to endure.

This is how our Heavenly Father treats us when we come back to Him, and this is what true sonship looks like. Every time someone returns home, Father throws open His arms, has a big party, celebrates, and restores *everything* back to them and they happily receive it all with gratitude. What a great Father we have!

So, you see that even if we ourselves have done something to temporarily detach ourselves from God, He does not hesitate to receive us back when we are truly ready. It doesn't matter if it is something we have done or something that has been done to us, Father watches for us. He waits with open arms. He restores us, forgives us and calls us His own.

Identity

Most of us aren't certain *who* we are and often confuse our identity with what we *do* and how we spend our time. If you were asked by a stranger, "Who are you?" What would you say? Your answer would probably consist of your name, the fact that you're a mother, how many children you have and what you do for a career or job outside the home. With that in mind, my answer would be, "I'm Barbara, mother of four, a writer, blogger, free-lance publisher, prayer partner and spiritual mentor." What I have just done is defined myself by my roles, responsibilities and what I do. I haven't actually said *who* I am.

If I define myself by my roles and what I do, when those things change, it causes me to be unsettled and unsure of who I am. Our identity should not be defined by temporal things, but by eternal things. Indeed, our identity should be based on who God says we are, not on what this world dictates.

Our identity should be rooted deeply in the truth that we are daughters of God and dearly loved by Him. Because we have been washed in the blood of Jesus, we can now say that we are new creations—the old has gone and the completely new has come (2 Cor. 5:17). We are ambassadors for Christ (2 Cor. 5:20), joint heirs with Him (Romans 8:17), and slaves to righteousness (Romans 6:18). We are God's workmanship born anew (Eph. 2:10), fearfully and wonderfully made by Him (Psalm 139:14), fully redeemed and made righteous in His sight (Eph. 4:24) and citizens of heaven seated in heavenly places (Eph. 2:6, Phil. 3:20). If someone asks *who* we are, our answer can simply be, "I am a woman of God, daughter of the King, dearly loved and highly favored." This is our identity, based on our relationship to God, and it is never going to change.

I remember when my youngest two children started school full-time; I experienced a crisis of identity. I had been a stay-at-home mom caring for young children for eight years straight and I had allowed it to become my identity and to completely consume me. I didn't know who I was without it. During the day when I was alone, I had to figure out who I was and where I would focus my energy. Our roles, responsibilities, and occupations *say* something about who we are as they reveal our passions, but at the core, we are simply daughters of the most-high God.

Beloved, if we trust God there is no need to fear the changes and the shifting happening in our families as our children grow and spread their wings. There should be no need to hang on for dear life to our sons or even our daughters. Over our lifetime, our roles will change and the way we connect with our children needs to change as they grow. We can't treat a five-year-old the same as a twelve-year-old and we can't treat a twelve-year-old the same as a twenty-year-old. Our relationship with our twenty-year-old is not the same as our relationship with our five-year-old. Being a mother needs to be thought of as a role that changes, not as an identity. In fact, if you think of being a mother as your identity, you will continue in it and try to *mother* (control) your adult children, to everyone's misery. At the very least, this will cause strife in your relationship with them and may even cause them to cut you out of their lives all together.

May your *identity* not be wrapped up in the role of motherhood, instead, may your *identity* be rooted in your relationship with Christ and being a daughter of the King. Your Heavenly Father is never going to leave you or forsake you. You will always be His and He will always be yours, no matter how mature you or your children become, nor how many years go by. There will be no crisis of identity when we put our roots down in Christ, where they belong.

Relationship Hindrances

There are a few things that could interfere with our ability to perceive and experience our Father/daughter relationship with God. They are:

- not being *wanted* by our earthly parents. Possibly we were unplanned or unexpected, abused, given up for adoption or conceived in rape.
- a pattern of rejection in our lives by others and ourselves.
- pinning after *lesser lovers*—specifically the approval of others.
- being angry at God—blaming Him for bad things happening to us.
- being mistreated by our earthly fathers.

Not Being Wanted

Have you ever felt like you have a *kick me* sign on your back? Have you struggled to let go of a sense of inferiority or not being good enough? If you have answered *yes* to either of these questions, you may need to come out of agreement with a belief that you were not wanted.

You may say, "But I *wasn't* wanted! I was given up for adoption." Indeed, it may be true that you weren't wanted by your biological parents, but beloved, it really doesn't matter. You *were* wanted by your heavenly Father. In fact, according to Ephesians 1:4-6, you were chosen by God before the creation of the world to be holy and blameless in His sight and you were predestined to be adopted as His daughter through Jesus. According to Psalm 139, the Lord has searched you and known you completely and He was the One who created your inmost being and knit you together in your mother's womb. So, why are we putting more importance on being wanted by earthly parents than being wanted and even chosen by God? Isn't that what we're doing if we choose to stay in a mindset of not being wanted? I encourage you today, right now, to come out of that mindset and to reject the lie that the enemy wants to hold you in. Based on the Word of God, His now prophetic word for you is:

> "Your earthly parents may not have planned you, but I did," says the Lord. "I chose you before the foundations of the world and I chose and planned who you would be and where and when you would be born. You were My choice, and you are My beloved. There was no mistake there, only My brilliant, intentional creativity. I knit you together in your mother's womb and I celebrate who you were then and who you are now; you are unique, you are amazing, you are My masterpiece, and you are Mine. You are my creative expression and I have put My Glory in you. Love yourself as I have loved you. You were wanted and you still are wanted by Me. I love you," says the Lord of Hosts.

I pray that you receive this word from the Lord and that it touches your heart.

I would encourage you to forgive your earthly parents if they hurt you in any way and pray a prayer something like this, out loud:

> "I renounce the lie that I was not wanted, and I confess that I was wanted and planned by my Heavenly Father. He knit me together in my mother's womb and I was fearfully and wonderfully made by Him. I choose to value God's acceptance over the acceptance of the world, and I choose to value God's love for me over the love in the world. I confess that God has wonderful plans for my life; plans to prosper me and not to harm me, plans to give me hope and a future (Jer. 29:11). In Jesus' name, Amen."

When praying the prayers included in this book, please remember that they are just guides and that simply reciting a prayer is powerless. Instead, we must bring our heart into agreement with the prayer first, be convinced of what we're praying and pray in faith for it to be effective. I would encourage you not to skip the prayers as Revelation 12:11 says, "They triumphed over him (the enemy) by the blood of the Lamb and by the word of their testimony" (bracket added). Speak the prayers out of your mouth and make them your testimony (confession) today.

Rejection

Very closely related to a sense of *not being wanted*, is a sense of rejection. For many women, rejection has played out in their lives in many ways and *not being wanted* was just the first experience with it. Many were bullied, made fun of or called names. Others were ignored, spoken *about* like they weren't even there, ditched by friends, dumped by boyfriends, neglected by a husband, divorced, or even left at the altar. It can be a very harsh world!

There are many ways that we can experience rejection, but what they all have in common is a message that convinces us, *we're not good enough*. This of course is a lie from the enemy in direct opposition to the truth of who we really are. Any time we agree with a lie of the devil, instead of believing the truth of God's Word, we give the devil power over us, and we need to repent, turn away from it and choose to change our minds about it.

I would encourage you to take inventory. Make a list of all the times you *felt* rejected by someone and forgive them. Realize that they simply did not see your worth and it's likely that they also have been affected at some point in their lives by rejection. In fact, those who have been rejected are very often the ones that reject others.

In addition, rejection causes the wounded to wear *rejection lenses*; it causes them to see *everything* as rejection. Perhaps they notice on Facebook that two of their friends went out to the movies and they immediately feel rejected because they weren't invited. They don't even think about the fact that none of the others in that group of friends were invited either and all they need to do is pick up the phone to invite someone else out. We don't have to sit back and wait for someone to invite us. We can take the initiative and invite someone else to do something fun with us.

Lastly, beloved, have you rejected yourself? When was the last time you gave yourself some love? Matthew 22:37-39 says:

> Jesus replied: "'Love the Lord your God with all your heart and with all your soul and with all your mind.' This is the first and greatest commandment. And the second is like it: 'Love your neighbor as yourself.'

We cannot love others well when we don't love ourselves first.

Here is a prayer of confession to experience the healing touch of the Lord:

> "Lord, I love You and give You praise for who You are. I confess to You right now that I have rejected myself, not liked myself or the way You have made me. I confess that I believed lies about who I am. I repent God and I ask You to forgive me now. I know that You have made me and that You have chosen me to be Yours and that everything You have made is very good. I am sorry that I have dishonored Your creation and not appreciated it. Thank You for Your forgiveness. Lord, give me eyes to see myself as You see me. In Jesus' name I renounce all self-hatred and self-rejection right now and I choose to love myself as You love me. I also come to You God in need of

healing. There are times when I have felt rejected by others and I need Your touch. I confess to You God that I have worshipped at the altar of man's opinion, and I repent for allowing the opinions of others to rule my experience. I also repent for rejecting others, pushing them away and hurting them. Forgive me Lord. I know Lord that You have never rejected me, and never will. You paid the ultimate price for me; You gave me all that You had, to save me and restore our relationship together. Help me Lord not to rely on other people for my emotional well-being, but to rely on Your unconditional love. Help me to be secure in You. Thank You for Your forgiveness and Your acceptance; I now see that just because other people have failed to love me well and see my worth does not make me worthless or un-lovely. With Your help, I will no longer allow other people to determine my worth. I know who I am in You Lord; I know that I am priceless in Your eyes. I now renounce rejection, I cut all ties to the spirit of rejection, and I command it, in the authority and power of Christ given to me according to Luke 10:19, to leave me alone and not come back. I choose to look to You God, my Heavenly Father, for my acceptance and validation and I decree that rejection no longer has any hold on my life, on my emotions or on my ability to relate to other people or God as my Father. Thank You, Father, that in Your Son, Jesus, I have freedom from rejection. Those the Son has set free are free indeed. Holy Spirit fill me up—fill every place in me that has been vacated, release Your power in me and make me whole in You. In Jesus' mighty name, Amen"

Pinning After Lesser Lovers: The Approval of Man

We've already talked a lot about our need for love and our tendency to look for love in all the wrong places. We want an easy, quick fix, so we try to get our love needs met through various things we can see and touch rather than straight from our divine source. These things end up becoming *lesser lovers,* meeting part of our need quickly, but never bringing lasting satisfaction. I've done it and I'm positive you have too; it is part of the human condition.

A close cousin to our need for love is our need for validation and approval. Unfortunately, most of us end up looking to other people for this and allowing their approval or disapproval to make or break us. We experience rejection because of this very mistake. We perform to please others, hungry for them to like us and prove to us that we are important.

When we live for the approval of man, our cycle of disappointment and rejection has no end, and it further removes us from the affections of Jesus we so desperately need. Beloved, decide today to put an axe to the root of the need for approval; it's not who you are, and you don't need it when you know who you are. It breaks God's heart, and it will break your heart repeatedly. Begin to receive, treasure, and honor the approval you already have from God as His beloved daughter.

Pray with me:

> "Lord God, I confess that I have been striving after the approval of others and I repent. Forgive me Lord, for valuing their approval above Yours, God. Forgive me for not seeing and not appropriately honoring Your approval. I receive Your forgiveness, love and acceptance now and I command my soul to be content

and to rest in our love relationship together, in Jesus' name, Amen."

Self-Reflection

As we wrap up this section, let me leave you with a few questions to reflect on:

1. How often do you communicate with your adult son?
2. Do you feel it is often enough or do you struggle with disappointment about not talking to him more often?
3. If you feel it's not often enough, how often do you *want* to communicate with your adult son and why?
4. How much of your striving and need for communication with him is due to your need for approval and validation from him?

Being Angry at God

One sure fire way to hinder your relationship with God is to harbor anger, resentment and/or offence towards God. These feelings and attitudes of the heart are many times not obvious for Christians (we hide them well) and require some self-reflection to identify. However, once revealed they are easy to deal with.

What causes these ill feelings towards God? Christians who are angry with God usually have suffered somehow at the hands of a perpetrator or due to a natural disaster. They know that God is sovereign, and they can't understand why God would *allow* their suffering. They ask themselves, *If God is good, all powerful and if He loves me, why didn't He intervene and prevent what was done?* This is an excellent question and understandably many contend with it for a long time. S*ome* of us who think that we've moved on and gotten over it, really haven't; we have just become experts at burying our pain deep inside. Some wear masks, smiling and pretending to be ok and some turn right away from God all together. Both have happened in my own family.

I believe the antidote for understanding why bad things happen to those who have believed on Christ, without blaming God, is a complete holistic understanding of the sovereignty of God. In an attempt to put the pieces together, let's first look at Genesis 1:28:

> God blessed them and said to them, "Be fruitful and increase in number; fill the earth and subdue it. Rule over the fish in the sea and the birds in the sky and over every living creature that moves on the ground."

Also consider Psalm 115:16, "The highest heavens belong to the Lord, but the earth he has given to mankind."

In Genesis 1:28, the word *subdue* is translated from the Hebrew word *kabash*, which means *to conquer, bring into subjection, force, and dominate*. We understand from these scriptures that God sovereignly assigned to man the management of the earth on His behalf. Man became His representative and intercessor. This is further confirmed by Ezekiel 22:30 which says:

> "I look for someone among them who would build up the wall and stand before me in the gap on behalf of the land so I would not have to destroy it, but I found no one.

Unfortunately, when Adam and Eve were deceived into doubting the Word of God, they fell into sin and forfeited their authority on this earth to the devil. From that point on, Satan became the god of this world (2 Cor. 4:4). Jesus then came, as a man to the earth and through His death and resurrection, reinstated the authority back to man, but unfortunately the devil is still here trying to deceive us; he is successfully influencing the world systems and those who have not yet surrendered to

Christ. We, as lovers of God and believers on Jesus are not *of* the world but are still *in* the world and are still being affected by the sin that still reigns here through unbelievers. It stinks, but it's true. The good news is Jesus has overcome the world and everything in it. We can take refuge in the knowledge that when we go through painful things, the Lord is right there with us and He will take what the enemy meant for harm, somehow turn it for good and heal our hearts of trauma, if we will let Him.

> "I have told you these things, so that in me you may have peace. In this world you will have trouble. But take heart! I have overcome the world." (John 16:33)

> And we know that in all things God works for the good of those who love him, who have been called according to his purpose. (Romans 8:28)

> And the God of all grace, who called you to his eternal glory in Christ, after you have suffered a little while, will himself restore you and make you strong, firm and steadfast. (1 Peter 5:10)

Beloved, the rock-bottom truth that we must stand firmly on is this: God loves us, God is for us and not against us and absolutely God is GOOD, ALL the time. If we can keep this in our minds: God = good and Satan = bad, we are less likely to get confused as to who caused our pain and who to blame.

We all know that God did not make mankind to be puppets or robots; He made us with free will and the ability to choose. When someone decides for themselves that they are going to act maliciously and sin against us, that is on them not God. Satan may have had a part to play, but ultimately, they have decided for themselves to act badly and sin against us. So, let's give credit where credit is due. Let's not blame God because it *appeared* that He didn't try to intervene. God knew ahead of time that His attempts to intervene would be ignored so instead, He remained with you, cried with you, and planned to redeem you.

You may think, *well, God could have just caused that person to drop dead before he/she could hurt me!* That is true, but *that* would mean that that person would die in their sin. God's heart is to give *everyone* opportunity to repent before they die as it's God's desire that ALL would come to repentance (2 Peter 3:9). So, God allows you to be hurt knowing that He is quite able to restore you and continues to draw the other person to repentance so they too can have their eternal home in heaven with Him. God loves them just as much as He loves you friend.

Being angry or offended with God is misguided and is simply corrected by recognizing if anger and offense is indeed in your heart, confessing it to God, turning away from it and receiving His forgiveness. Voicing forgiveness towards God in prayer along with the previous steps, will complete the process and ensure your freedom.

Here's a prayer that will help. Remember to bring your heart into agreement with what you are saying:

> "Lord God, I confess that I have wrongly blamed You for (name specifically what happened; if there is more than one circumstance, name them separately). I am sorry. Please forgive me. I know that You would not do anything simply to hurt me or make my life miserable. That is not Your heart. I know that You want only the best for me and my family. Thank You for Your forgiveness. Lord, please heal my heart of the pain that I still feel about this event/loss. Reveal to me how You felt about the loss God. Show me Your heart, God, and show me where You were when this event took place; I know You were with me; it is Your Word (pause and let God speak to you). Thank You, Jesus.

Thank You, God, that You were just as grieved as I was over it. Just as You wept at the tomb of Lazarus, even though You knew he would live again, You wept over my loss as well. Thank You for Your love. (If you blame anyone else, forgive them here, if you have not already done so.) In the name of Jesus and the authority He has given me, I now bind any spirit of trauma that may have found a home in me because of this event. I pull it out of every cell of my body, and I command it to leave me now, in Jesus' name. I decree that I am free from trauma and free to know and experience God as my heavenly Father. Holy Spirit come and fill me up to overflowing; invade every space that has been emptied. Fill every part of my heart, spirit, soul, and body. In Jesus' mighty name, amen."

Bad Experiences with Earthly Fathers

Our experiences with our earthly fathers can skew our beliefs about and trust in our heavenly Father as we project our hurt feelings onto all fathers; our expectations are set according to our experiences in the past. I remember a time when I was young, my mother was about to take me out to get new boots for the winter and my father was angry that she was about to spend more money. In his mind, it was unnecessary, as we had many pairs of boots from previous years that I should have been able to wear. I'm sure he was just overwhelmed with the expenses of a family of five, but I couldn't understand how he expected me to wear boots that were too small, and I was hurt that he didn't seem to want to provide for my needs.

I projected this experience with my earthly father onto God and it caused me to see God as stingy, angry about providing for me and reluctant to do so. The truth about God is the complete opposite; He is overjoyed to provide abundantly for His children (Phil. 4:19, John 10:10, Matt. 6:28-30, 2 Cor. 9:8).

There's a beautiful song on YouTube by Misty Edwards called, *All Men Are Broken,* that will soak your soul in love and truth as you listen. She is an incredibly anointed minister of prophetic song. Go find it right now and receive truth and healing into your heart. Let yourself feel what you need to feel and let it go; forgive your father, release him, and receive Father God deeper than you ever have before. You are deeply loved, and Papa God is turning it all around for you. You'll see—He's not forgotten anything.

If you've submitted to God and allowed the Holy Spirit to work in you over the previous challenges, you should begin to feel closer in your connection with the Lord. If you have had trouble connecting with the prayers or allowing the Holy Spirit to work things out in you, seek some help from a pastor or a trusted, mature Christian friend. Sometimes it's difficult to allow ourselves to crack open; it can be painful and it's easier just to let things be as they are.

Perhaps you are even surprised at how much I am attempting to get into your business. This is not what you signed up for! Perhaps you thought this book was going to be just a light read you could skim over. If so, sorry. I'm not good at writing fluff and I can't stand living a life coasting on leftovers or anything less than the fullness and abundance God intended. I'm going after it all! I hope you are joining me.

I pray that you have come to a place where you are experiencing, to a greater measure, a fulfilling father/daughter relationship with God. I pray that in days ahead this spiritual reality will begin to be seen more and more in your daily life, in the way you plan your day, spend your time, trust God with your needs and interact with your children.

One final Word to bless your heart:

For the Lord your God is living among you. He is a mighty savior. He will take delight in you with gladness. With his love, he will calm all your fears. He will rejoice over you with joyful songs." (Zeph. 3:17, NLT)

From Daughter to Bride

*J*ust when you've taken a deeper dive, experienced God like never before and partaken of more, I need to tell you, it is possible and even expected that you would go even deeper. For a long time, you've been satisfied with just being wet, splashing around in the kiddie pool, but now there is an ocean of intimacy before you waiting to be experienced and explored.

Just as a human relationship deepens and grows in intimacy, going from acquaintances to friends and then perhaps to best friends, and just as another certain relationship may turn into commitment, engagement, marriage and passionate love, our relationship with God can also grow in intimacy the same way. We first think of ourselves as a servant of God, then His friend. As our relationship with God grows, hopefully we become His daughter and finally His lover and bride. Each level of intimacy and love manifests into deeper commitment, passion, and fervor to know, experience and please all three persons Who are God (Father, Son and Holy Spirit). Don't be surprised when your life looks totally different as you fall deeper and deeper in love with Him.

Does it toy with your mind, thinking of God as your lover? Does it make you squirm? If it does, you're not the only one. We are used to thinking of a lover as someone with whom we have sex, as we confuse love with sex all the time, but let's be real—they are not synonymous. We do not have sex with everyone that we love and having sex does not automatically mean love—unfortunately, some of us found that out the hard way.

Just as a farm-er is simply someone who farms, a lov-er is someone who loves, and love can be expressed in many different ways. As humans we *can* express love by having sex, but that is not what we're talking about here. However, we *are* talking about love being expressed through *intimacy*, which can be simply thought of as *in-to-me-see*. Intimacy is about knowing someone, knowing their heart, their deepest desires, and their deepest fears. It's when someone knows what we are going to say even before we say it. One of my most favorite passages of scripture reads:

> Lord, you know everything there is to know about me. You perceive every movement of my heart and soul, and you understand my every thought before it even enters my mind. You are so intimately aware of me, Lord. You read my heart like an open book and you know all the words I'm about to speak before I even start a sentence! You know every step I will take before my journey even begins. You've gone into my future to prepare the way, and in kindness you follow behind me to spare me from the harm of my past. You have laid your hand on me! (Psalm 139:1-5, TPT)

How wonderful and truly comforting to have someone who knows us so completely, and even still, loves us so deeply! We will never ever be misunderstood or falsely accused of anything by the Lord. He knows our heart inside and out. He is truly trustworthy, and we can fully rest in His complete, everlasting love.

Part of the beauty of intimacy with the Lord is that it works both ways. He not only knows us deeply, but we can get to know His heart deeply as well. When we honor Him and spend time with Him, He begins to share His most treasured thoughts and secrets with us and we get to know what He loves and what He hates, what He longs for and even what His plans may be. Jeremiah 33:3 says, "Call to me and I will answer you and tell you great and unsearchable things you do not know."

When we know God's heart well, we will have the ability to discern between our own soulish thoughts, thoughts coming from God's heart and thoughts coming from the devil and this my friend, is a tremendous help in navigating life. Paying attention to our thoughts and exercising discernment pays off. We can then completely avoid all the traps that Satan lays for us or tries to get us entangled with, and that right there deserves a hallelujah!

There are many scriptures that reference God and Jesus being our husband, redeemer, and bridegroom. In the Old Testament we start with Isaiah 54:4-6:

> "Do not be afraid; you will not be put to shame. Do not fear disgrace; you will not be humiliated. You will forget the shame of your youth and remember no more the reproach of your widowhood. For your Maker is your husband – the Lord Almighty is his name – the Holy One of Israel is your Redeemer; He is called the God of all the earth.

This passage is speaking about the city of Jerusalem or Zion, but very much includes the people of the area and all those who would be grafted into the people of God—you and me. Go back, read it again, meditate on it and hear the Lord speak it into your heart this very moment.

When the fall happened with Adam and Eve, as said earlier, we were banished from the garden, and we *died* to God. God *did* warn Adam and Eve ahead of time, that they would "surely die" (Gen. 2:17) when they ate of that tree. We became orphans, but it was also as if we became widows as well. We lost our husband—the One who loved us perfectly, protected us and cared for us. Suddenly, we became in need of a savior and a redeemer.

God did not leave us banished but sent Jesus to redeem us. *Redeem,* according to dictionary.com means to "buy or pay off; clear by payment, to buy back, to recover, to exchange, to convert, to discharge or fulfill, to make up for; make amends for; offset, to obtain the release or restoration of, as from captivity, by paying a ransom and to deliver from sin and its consequences by means of a sacrifice offered for the sinner." In the Old Testament, if a woman's husband died, his brother or close family member was expected to re-marry her and redeem her from her widowhood—to vindicate her, rescue her and to remove from her the disgrace and shame of being alone. This family member was called a *Kinsman Redeemer.*

The story of Ruth and Boaz in the Bible gives us a beautiful example of how a Kinsman Redeemer blesses a family and rescues widows. It is also a profound illustration of what Jesus has done for us. Perhaps you know the story but let me set it up for you.

There was a famine in the land, so a man from Bethlehem named Elimelek, his wife Noami and their two sons went to Moab in search of a better life. After a short time passed,

Elimelek unfortunately died. The two sons both married Moabite women, Orpah and Ruth, but not long after that, both sons also died leaving all three women alone, without their husbands.

Eventually, Naomi heard that the famine in her homeland had ended, so the three women prepared to leave Moab and return to Judah. Shortly after they began their journey, Naomi had a change of heart and urged her daughters-in-law to return to Moab and their original families, so they could possibly find new husbands. Orpah agreed and turned back, but Ruth refused. Ruth insisted on staying with Noami. In this well known, beautiful passage of scripture, Ruth expresses her desire to accept the one true God as her God and to remain with Naomi whom she had come to love:

> But Ruth replied, "Don't urge me to leave you or to turn back from you. Where you go I will go, and where you stay I will stay. Your people will be my people and your God my God. (Ruth 1:16)

Loyal and courageous Ruth refuses to go back to what is familiar and recognizes the road she's on with Naomi is beautiful and blessed. She loves her mother-in-law and stays connected with the new family the Lord directed her to. Ruth sees the benefits of entering the new and chooses to go forward instead of backwards, up the path laid out before her by God, despite it being unknown to her. I'm sure she also knows Naomi can't travel alone, so stays to help her.

After arriving in Bethlehem, they needed food, so Ruth decided to glean behind the harvesters in one of the nearby fields. Unbeknownst to her, she ends up gleaning in the field of a relative of Noami's late husband, who happens to be an eligible Kinsman Redeemer for their family. And there's God, once again orchestrating what only He can! Here's the story from Ruth chapter 2:

> So she went out, entered a field and began to glean behind the harvesters. As it turned out, she was working in a field belonging to Boaz, who was from the clan of Elimelek. Just then Boaz arrived from Bethlehem and greeted the harvesters, "The Lord be with you!" "The Lord bless you!" they answered. Boaz asked the overseer of his harvesters, "Who does that young woman belong to?" The overseer replied, "She is the Moabite who came back from Moab with Noami. She said, 'Please let me glean and gather among the sheaves behind the harvesters.' She came into the field and has remained here from morning till now, except for a short rest in the shelter." So Boaz said to Ruth, "My daughter, listen to me. Don't go and glean in another field and don't go away from here. Stay here with the women who work for me. Watch the field where the men are harvesting, and follow along after the women. I have told the men not to lay a hand on you. And whenever you are thirsty, go and get a drink from the water jars the men have filled." At this, she bowed down with her face to the ground. She asked him, "Why have I found such favor in your eyes that you notice me – a foreigner?" Boaz replied, "I've been told all about what you have done for your mother-in-law since the death of your husband – how you left your father and mother and your homeland and came to live with a people you did not know before. May the Lord repay you for what you have done. May you be richly rewarded by the Lord, the God of Israel, under whose wings you have come to take refuge." (Ruth 2:3-12)

And from there, the favor over Ruth continued until Boaz took her as his wife. It's such a beautiful story of redemption, going from desolation to complete fullness in every way, even to the point of bearing a son in the lineage of Jesus.

This is the same favor, our Kinsman Redeemer, Jesus, lavishes over us—even when we're foreigners. He blesses us like a Godly husband, a strong protector, guardian, and provider.

John the Baptist also refers to Jesus as the bridegroom in John chapter 3:

> You yourselves can testify that I said, 'I am not the Messiah but am sent ahead of him.' The bride belongs to the bridegroom. The friend who attends the bridegroom waits and listens for him, and is full of joy when he hears the bridegroom's voice. That joy is mine, and it is now complete. He must become greater; I must become less." (John 3:28-30)

Jesus also uses a wedding analogy to describe the kingdom of heaven in Matthew 25:

> "At that time the kingdom of heaven will be like ten virgins who took their lamps and went out to meet the bridegroom. Five of them were foolish and five were wise. The foolish ones took their lamps but did not take any oil with them. The wise ones, however, took oil in jars along with their lamps. The bridegroom was a long time in coming, and they all became drowsy and fell asleep. At midnight the cry rang out: 'Here's the bridegroom! Come out to meet him!' "Then all the virgins woke up and trimmed their lamps. The foolish ones said to the wise, 'Give us some of your oil; our lamps are going out.' "'No,' they replied, 'there may not be enough for both us and you. Instead, go to those who sell oil and buy some for yourselves.' "But while

they were on their way to buy the oil, the bridegroom arrived. The virgins who were ready went in with him to the wedding banquet. And the door was shut. "Later the others also came. 'Lord, Lord,' they said, 'open the door for us!' "But he replied, 'Truly I tell you, I don't know you.' "Therefore keep watch, because you do not know the day or the hour. (Matthew 25:1-13)

This parable is the most poignant of all for us right now, to understand how we need to be ready to receive our Bridegroom, Jesus, when He returns. You will notice that *all* ten of the ladies were virgins—meaning they were all pure, righteous, and holy, cleansed in the blood of Jesus, however, only five were prepared and ready for the Bridegroom's arrival.

There are a few things that we can see from this parable that seem simple at first glance but provide important prophetic insight. First, notice that the Bridegroom comes at nighttime when it's dark, as each virgin had to have a lamp that was shining. This is not necessarily telling us that Jesus will come back at nighttime when it is naturally dark, but more likely that He comes back amidst spiritual darkness.

Secondly, each virgin had to have her own lamp. Recently when reading this parable, I remembered as a young person navigating the paths at night while at camp, with a flashlight. It wasn't uncommon for some of us to walk together as not everyone had their own flashlight. It struck me that the virgins who didn't have extra oil could not share the light of the wise virgins. Each of us, when Christ returns, will need to be shining brightly with our *own* light, as we were designed to do.

> "You are the light of the world. A town built on a hill cannot be hidden. Neither do people light a lamp and put it under a bowl. Instead they put it on its stand, and it gives light to everyone in the house. In the same way, let your light shine before others, that they may see

your good deeds and glorify your Father in heaven. (Matt. 5:14-16)

Thirdly, in order for the virgins' lamps to burn, they needed extra oil. The question then becomes, "What does the oil represent?" This is the most important question as it was the primary difference between the wise and the unwise—between the ones that entered the wedding feast and the ones who were locked out. I believe the answer lies in the Bridegroom's statement to the unwise, "Truly I tell you, I don't know you" (v.12).

I have heard many say that the oil represents the Holy Spirit, but I would suggest that the oil represents intimacy. We only truly shine when we have been filled up in the secret place with the affections of God. You, along with the presence of the Holy Spirit inside you are the lamp, and the oil of intimacy causes you to burn with love for Jesus. Let's make sure we deal with everything that hinders or blocks our intimacy with Him.

Forgiveness

I suspect most of you, my beloved readers, are aware that salvation is a gift from God. Romans 6:23 says, "For the wages of sin is death, but the gift of God is eternal life in Christ Jesus our Lord," and Ephesians 2:8&9 says, "For it is by grace you have been saved, through faith – and this is not from yourselves, it is the gift of God – not by works, so that no one can boast." Although salvation is free, it is not without cost. Indeed, in Luke 14:33, Jesus tells us that it will cost us everything. "In the same way, those of you who do not give up everything you have cannot be my disciples." Whatever you are not willing to give up for Christ will block your fellowship and intimacy with Him.

Everything. Let that sink in for a minute. Everything includes *everything*—your heart, your family, your marriage, your children, your life, your time, your finances, your comfort, your reputation, your _____. You fill in the blank. Are you feeling uncomfortable yet? Does this mean Jesus wants us to have nothing, to be broke and lonely, desperate, and destitute? No, it absolutely does not. It means He wants our single wholehearted devotion. He wants us to love Him first and foremost, out of everything and everyone in our lives. We must trust Him with everything we have. We must be willing to allow Him to remove from us or prune whatever is hindering our relationship with Him. It requires open hands and not clenched fists. It requires us not to hang on to anything too tight.

This *everything* that Jesus talks about also includes our wounds and our rights—our rights to justice, our rights to an apology where appropriate and all our *you owe me(s)* that we've accumulated and kept track of over the years from all the ones who have hurt us. This *everything* requires us to lay down *everything* and forgive the offences against us. According to Matthew 6:15, if we don't, we will not be forgiven by our Heavenly Father. "But if you do not forgive others their sins, your Father will not forgive your sins."

Jesus tells a parable in Matthew 18:23-35 about an unmerciful servant which clearly illustrates to us that the forgiveness we have received from the Lord, we must also offer to others in turn.

> "Therefore, the kingdom of heaven is like a king who wanted to settle accounts with his servants. As he began the settlement, a man who owed him ten thousand bags of gold was brought to him. Since he was not able to pay, the master ordered that he and his wife and his children and all that he had be sold to repay the debt.

"At this the servant fell on his knees before him, 'Be patient with me,' he begged, 'and I will pay back everything.' The servant's master took pity on him, canceled the debt and let him go.

"But when that servant went out, he found one of his fellow servants who owed him a hundred silver coins. He grabbed him and began to choke him, 'Pay back what you owe me!' he demanded.

"His fellow servant fell to his knees and begged him, 'Be patient with me, and I will pay it back.'

"But he refused. Instead, he went off and had the man thrown into prison until he could pay the debt. When the other servants saw what had happened, they were outraged and went and told their master everything that had happened.

"Then the master called the servant in. 'You wicked servant,' he said, 'I canceled all that debt of yours because you begged me to. Shouldn't you have had mercy on your fellow servant just as I had on you?' In anger his master handed him over to the jailers to be tortured, until he should pay back all he owed.

"This is how my heavenly Father will treat each of you unless you forgive your brother or sister from your heart." (Matthew 18:23-35)

The King cancelled our debt, now we must cancel the debts of others lest we be handed over to the jailers and tormented. Like me, if you've ever gone through a time when you have held onto unforgiveness, you will know exactly what this means. Unforgiveness has a way of tormenting our minds with anger, bitterness and fear, our dreams with nightmares, our lives with unjust circumstances and even our bodies with illness. Much is released and set right when we finally agree to release those who have sinned against us, including our body, mind, heart, and intimacy with our heavenly Father.

What does forgiveness look like? It *doesn't* look like warm fuzzy feelings, and it doesn't look like getting back into relationship with toxic people. It *does* look like making a simple choice. Simple, but not necessarily easy.

The first step includes making up our mind to release someone and what they have done to us. I always suggest to people to be very specific and to pray out loud, bringing their heart into agreement with these words, "I choose to forgive (name the person who hurt you or offended you) for (name what they did and how they made you feel)." Make this your confession daily or as often as necessary, until your emotions come into alignment with your will.

If you are having trouble with this, ask the Lord to help you. Confess to Him that you want to forgive, but you don't know how. Pray and wait on the Lord until you can say you forgive them with sincerity; His grace will come and help you as you lean on Him.

Once we have decided to forgive and let things go, we must continue in that decision. This means not allowing ourselves to dwell on the situation further or rehash it over and over within ourselves or with others. We must use self-control to continually choose to let it go. If you find yourself thinking about it again and/or thinking badly about the person who is responsible, say out loud again, "I choose to forgive (name the person) for (name what they did and how they made you feel)."

Lastly, begin to pray for the individual. Start with simply asking the Lord to bless them. As your emotions heal and come into agreement with your will, you will be able to pray even more. Ask the Holy Spirit to lead you and show you how to pray for them. Additionally, ask the Holy Spirit to show you their heart and what they struggle with in order to pray with compassion and empathy.

Emotional Healing

In addition to voicing our choice to forgive someone, it is incredibly healing for us to recognize our feelings surrounding the wounds inflicted by others and give them to God. We have been stuffing our feelings and emotions for far too long and they could be making us sick. Our feelings are valid, and they should be recognized and expressed in a healthy way. In addition, I have learned over the last while that the exercise of validating our feelings and releasing them to God becomes so much more profound when we are willing to engage with God through our imaginations. Let me explain.

Our mind and imagination were given to us by God, and they were never intended by God to be used for ungodly purposes. In fact, God speaks to us through them all the time—unfortunately however, we don't recognize it. We think the random ideas that come to us or the thoughts that seem to just spontaneously pop into our minds is us, but very often it's not; many times, it's God. God loves to speak to us, and we would experience more harmony and blessing in our lives if we would begin to recognize His voice and allow Him to give us pictures on the screen of our imagination. Do you remember my testimony about the children and Jesus coming to greet us, from page 49-50? The Lord did that all on the screen of my imagination and if I had not been open to receive from God in that way, I may not have been healed in my heart and my emotions that day.

Now you and I both know, and I hear some of you saying this now, *"But our imaginations can't be trusted."* You're right. We must be careful but let me explain how we can receive from the

Lord, without being misled. I really don't want you to miss out on this amazing experience with God.

All of us were born into a sinful nature and all of us have used our imagination for vain purposes and in ungodly ways. We have all fantasized about something we probably shouldn't have. Yes? Incidentally, just in case you don't know, fantasizing about anyone other than your husband is sin; please be careful about what you read and watch as it doesn't take much to trigger ungodly fantasy. Some movies rated R and even some rated PG-13 and 18+ are too much for some of us, me included (Matt. 5:28). Have you given into temptation? Curiosity? Has anyone seen *Magic Mike*? *Fifty Shades of Grey*? How did they affect your mind? I bet it has taken you a long time to stop thinking about it. Lust has a way of gripping our minds and not letting go. Thankfully, our sin is easily dealt with through confession and repentance, and I submit to you right now, that you can push the reset button on your imagination and decide to set it apart for Godly purposes from here on out.

We can, at will, imagine *anything* we want to. Can't we? There is no limit to where we can go. Our mind is an amazing and powerful organ and tool, but it is completely our choice how to use it and fill it. When we are free through confession, repentance, and the blood of Jesus, no one and nothing can force us to imagine something we don't want to imagine—so make the choice. Make the choice today to submit and set apart your imagination for God and God alone. Make the choice to renew your mind with God's Word and to fill your mind with only Godly things.

Pray a prayer like this:

> "Lord, I confess to You today that I have used my imagination for ungodly purposes, and I am sorry. I ask You to forgive me and cleanse me from all unrighteousness. I ask You, God, to cleanse my mind

and my imagination with the blood of Jesus and I choose right now to submit my imagination to You and set it apart for Your purposes. Help me Jesus to use wisdom in what I watch, what I read and how I fill my mind and imagination. In Jesus' name. Amen."

Here's a hint: begin to pay attention to how you feel, what you're thinking about and what you're imagining after watching something on TV or at the movie theatre. You may need to begin pruning away some things and being more selective with your entertainment. I even had to stop watching Grey's Anatomy as I noticed that I felt different after watching it—in a bad way.

Emotional Healing Exercise

Dr. Douglas E. Carr from *Doug Carr Freedom Ministries Inc.* taught us this technique in our deliverance training, and we use it quite often in *Healing Rooms* at my church. It creates an opportunity for us to recognize how we feel, name it, and release it to God, for real. Read right through the next part and get an understanding of the exercise before you begin. You'll want to do the exercise without having to break the flow.

Get in a quiet place with God, alone. Focus your mind on God and begin to admire Him and worship Him quietly in your heart. Pray:

"Lord, I thank You for my imagination. I thank You for Your blood that cleanses me and makes me whole. Lord, I invite You to speak to me through my imagination right now."

Make a bowl with your hands, close your eyes, and ask the Holy Spirit to remind you of the instances when you were hurt. If nothing comes to mind immediately, ask the Holy Spirit to bring a memory to your mind and wait for Him to speak. Don't question Him when He does. If it comes to your mind, there is something that needs to be healed.

Next, ask the Holy Spirit to show you how that event or that person made you feel. As He shows you, speak it out, "Lord, that person made me feel _____." As you speak out ALL the specific feelings and emotions surrounding the event, put it in the bowl, using your imagination. See in your mind's eye, you putting that feeling into the bowl that you've made with your hands. Keep your eyes closed the entire time. Continue to speak out all the ways you felt. Put them all in the bowl. Feel how heavy the bowl has become. Cry if you need to.

Next, with your eyes closed, on the screen of your imagination picture Jesus standing in front of you. See Him there. Focus on Him. What is He wearing? Notice the details if you can. What color are His eyes? Where are His hands? By faith, trust the Holy Spirit to speak to you through the pictures that come. At this point, the Holy Spirit is in control. Allow Him to speak and don't minimize what you see. Don't think that it's just you making it up. It's not. It's God.

As you see Jesus standing in front of you, hand Him the bowl. Give Jesus that heavy bowl, see Him take it and notice what He does with it. Notice and make a mental note, what does Jesus do with the bowl?

Nearly 100% of the time we do this exercise with people, they see something profound, and they weep. Sometimes this exercise doesn't work well because people don't allow themselves to be still and focused. Eliminating distractions from your environment will help. If you're having trouble "seeing" pictures, don't worry about it. Just allow God to do what He is doing. Some people struggle to get pictures but will get slight impressions in their mind.

The important thing is to give yourself permission to feel what you feel. Call it out, give it to Jesus and be healed.

Earthly Husband and Heavenly Husband

Are you married? If so, there's a good chance that you have practiced forgiveness a lot already. In fact, you may be an expert. Your marriage could very well be the one place where you need to forgive daily.

My husband and I have been married for thirty years and we absolutely need to communicate, confront, and forgive a lot—me him and the other way around as well. I certainly am not perfect either. I have learned that storing up frustration, hurt and disappointment is very damaging, not only to the marriage relationship, but also to our health. Take some time and process your feelings with God and with your husband. Once your husband knows clearly how you feel, he is responsible to God to make things right.

If there is disappointment and hurt feelings regarding intimacy with your husband, this could very well affect your expectations of and desire for intimacy with Jesus. It could cause you to withdraw or it could cause you to seek Him out even more fervently. Let it be the latter.

Examine your heart. Better yet, ask God to examine your heart and show you what's there. We can be experts at hiding our true feelings. Our hearts tend to hide things away in an attempt to protect us from emotional pain. Jeremiah 17:9 says, "The heart is deceitful above all things And it is extremely sick; Who can understand it fully and know its secret motives" (AMP)? The good news is that nothing is hidden from God. Be like King David when he prayed, "Search me, God, and know my heart; test me and know my anxious thoughts. See if there is any offensive way in me, and lead me in the way everlasting" (Psalm 139:23-24).

Beloved, your heavenly husband is not like your earthly husband. He's waaaay better! I don't mean any disrespect here. God bless you if you have a wonderful husband. I'm happy for you! Unfortunately, though, many women even while married suffer from great loneliness, rejection, and neglect. If that's you, beloved, rest in the truth that your heavenly husband knows you beyond knowing and loves you with perfect love. He is always encouraging, never critical and always wants to spend time with you. In fact, He waits for you with anticipation every moment of every day. He loves to hear your voice, loves to talk with you and listens intently to every word you say. He knows the number of hairs on your head, and He has engraved your name on the palm of His hand. He loves you as you have never been loved before.

Run to Him beloved; He waits with open arms. May you come to know His love, by experience, as you love and worship Him, in spirit and in truth.

Emotional Attachments

September 2006, our youngest two munchkins started school two to three days per week. Two years later, at the age of six, they started school full-time, and I no longer had children at home to care for during the day. It was weird and it was lonely. It felt unnatural for me, and I had to fight off the desire to have more children simply because I wanted to continue to nurture. It felt like there was a void in my life that needed to be filled.

As a result, Daisy became part of our family in October of 2010—a little white Bichon puppy who needed some tender loving care. If you've already got four kids and you still have a need to nurture, you may want to consider getting a pet instead of having another baby. Babies grow up and eventually go to school, leaving you alone again.

Although we welcomed Daisy into our home on Jessica's sixteenth birthday, if I'm being totally honest, I would admit

Daisy was more for me and my emotional health than she was for Jessica. I really enjoyed snuggling Daisy and having her company and she really enjoyed the belly rubs. Isn't it amazing how attached we can become to animals even with the limited amount of verbal communication we have with them.

Attachments obviously go beyond pets, and Godly attachments are good for our souls. We were designed by God to live in relationship with one another. Even God said it wasn't good for Adam to be alone. We have natural attachments to our spouse, children, extended family, friends, pastors, and others, but there are times when our attachments go deep, even to the intermingling and oneness of souls. One example of this is between a husband and a wife. They become one together in soul, bound and yoked together in covenant with each another. This bond is solidified physically when their marriage is consummated.

Another type of deep attachment can be between family members or friends whom we have come to love deeply with a brotherly type of love. One example of this from scripture was between King David and Jonathan, son of Saul. First Samuel 18:1&3 says, "Now when he had finished speaking to Saul, the soul of Jonathan was knit to the soul of David, and Jonathan loved him as his own soul... Then Jonathan and David made a covenant, because he loved him as his own soul" (NKJV*)*. King Saul had taken David into the palace to live, and Jonathan received him fully and graciously, taking him in like a brother.

These deep attachments are wonderful and remain Godly so long as love is our goal, which means we are focused on being a *giver* and not a *taker*. Remember 1 Corinthians 13:4-5?

> "Love is patient, love is kind. It does not envy, it does not boast, it is not proud. It does not dishonor others,

it is not self-seeking, it is not easily angered, it keeps no record of wrongs." (Emphasis mine)

As adults, attachments are Godly when we are focused on what we can *give* rather than on what we can *get* in a relationship. Unfortunately, our wounded souls don't always operate in Godly ways. We at times, can be needy, as we've already discussed, desperate for love and affirmation. A problem can arise when we rely too heavily on other people and even pets to meet our emotional needs. We end up taking and taking, and even relying on them, sometimes solely, putting unrealistic demands on them and putting them in an ungodly position they were not meant to occupy.

What happens when we have not stewarded a relationship well and we have allowed ourselves to make that person like God in our lives (ie. they have become our primary source of love) and they move or leave or shift away from us somehow? We feel threatened and we have unrealistic, exaggerated emotional responses because we need that person to feed us emotionally. When this happens, we put ourselves in a very vulnerable and ungodly position. We have given another person way too much power over us.

Every relationship has boundaries, and we must be aware of them and follow them. Unfortunately, boundaries can easily be crossed when we're desperate and not standing guard over our souls. We can so easily slip into ungodly territory.

Take for instance a marriage that is not functioning according to Godly parameters. A husband is withdrawn and not really interested in maintaining a connection with his wife after twenty years. He feels burnt out, tired and very much like a failure, just wanting to veg in front of the TV alone or withdrawing by himself into a hobby that he finds enjoyment in. He is desperately trying to avoid those things and people he feels like he has failed. His wife, who becomes desperate for male companionship and emotional connection, connects with the only other male who is readily available to her, living in her own household, without even realizing it. Her son becomes her confidant, her rock and the one to give her the encouragement she so desperately needs. In this situation, a boundary has been crossed and mom has put her son in a position that he was never meant to occupy.

Ladies, your son should never be your confidant, your rock or the one who meets your emotional needs. We can have close relationships with our sons, for sure. We can love them deeply, but don't ever be a taker in your relationship with him. He can give to you at his will, and we can receive, but don't ever expect him or rely on him to give. It's not his place or his responsibility; it is your husband's. If your husband is not fulfilling his God given role, you will need to pray and ask God how to speak to your husband about it and you will need to delve deeper into intimacy with Christ.

It's vital that God be our primary source of love, approval, and validation through an intimate connection with Him directly. After that, our husbands should be fulfilling their role as your emotional support and encouragement, allowing the love of God to flow through him to you. He's the one with flesh on, who should be a conduit for the love of God on your behalf, and vice versa. If he's not that for you, something needs to change; a crucial conversation needs to happen and perhaps counselling with a pastor or a professional. I will also warn you though, your husband is not God, and so he does need a lot of grace, just as we do. He is not perfect, he will make mistakes and he has his own wounds, habits and hang-ups to deal with. Hopefully, he's submitted to God just as you are, allowing the Lord to do His redemptive work in his heart as well.

Finally, the most important point in this whole book... Beloved, when we are hurt and lonely and the threat of losing someone we have come to depend on for love, affection, and support looms, what do we do? What is our normal, human reaction of the flesh when we are threatened with loss? We try to stop it! Right? We try to protect ourselves... And we do this by trying to control the situation. We try to control circumstances and we try to control and manipulate whoever is involved, in order to keep them close and where we need them to be. Beloved, is this you? Have you been trying to control? If so, the final questions and concerns here would be: Is it Godly? Is trying to control other people honoring? Is it righteous? Does it demonstrate *living by faith*? Does the need to control others demonstrate trust in God, or does it come from a root of fear? I hope you will agree, it is time to stop trying to control others and trust God to love us, to look after us and to cause good to come out of every situation.

Based on Isaiah 61, Jesus has come to declare the good news to the poor in spirit, those who have been crushed by loneliness and despair. He has come to bind up your broken heart, proclaim to you freedom from darkness, favor, vengeance on your behalf, to comfort you and provide for you. He stands ready to bestow on you a crown of beauty instead of ashes, the oil of joy instead of mourning and a garment of praise instead of a spirit of heaviness. You will be called an oak of righteousness, "a planting of the Lord for the display of his splendor" (Is.61:3).

> Instead of your shame you will receive a double portion, and instead of disgrace you will rejoice in your inheritance. And so you will inherit a double portion in your land, and everlasting joy will be yours.
>
> "For I, the Lord, love justice; I hate robbery and wrongdoing. In my faithfulness I will reward my

people and make an everlasting covenant with them. Their descendants will be known among the nations and their offspring among the peoples. All who see them will acknowledge that they are a people the Lord has blessed."

I delight greatly in the Lord; my soul rejoices in my God. For he has clothed me with garments of salvation and arrayed me in a robe of his righteousness, as a bridegroom adorns his head like a priest, and as a bride adorns herself with her jewels. (Isaiah 61:7-10)

If the Holy Spirit has tugged on your heart regarding an emotional reliance on your son and/or a tendency to control, below is a prayer that you can say out loud to repent and release yourself, and him, from an ungodly soul connection. Remember to bring your heart into agreement with what you are saying.

"Lord, I thank You for my son. I thank You that You have blessed our family with his life. I confess Lord, that I have put ungodly expectations on him. I have looked to him for the love and emotional support I needed, which I should have received from You or my husband. I repent God and I'm sorry that I did not seek You out to meet my needs. Forgive me God and cleanse me from all unrighteousness. I choose to forgive myself for putting my son in an ungodly position; I receive Your complete forgiveness Lord and I thank You for it. I now sever and renounce every ungodly connection and covenant I have made with my son and I cut the spiritual umbilical cord that has kept him attached to me long past the appropriate time. Lord, I ask You to cleanse every part of him that has been wrongly attached to me and I release it back to him now. Make him whole in You God. Also, I now call back to me, every part of myself that has been wrongly attached to my son. I pray God that You would cleanse that piece of my heart Lord and make me whole in You again. I ask You God to heal every wound in me that caused me to wrongly attach to my son and I ask You God to heal any wound in my son, which I may have caused. I now declare, in Jesus' name, that any curse that was empowered because of our ungodly union is broken now. I thank You Jesus, that You became a curse for us and that You took upon Yourself every curse of the law so that we both could be free. Lord, I also confess to You that I have attempted to control my son so that he would remain attached to me and love me beyond what is appropriate. I am sorry and I repent. I understand that attempting to control anyone is not godly and I ask You God to forgive me and reveal to me any other area or person I am attempting to control (pause and listen to the Holy Spirit; confess and repent for anything He shows you). Lord God, I also confess to You that I have been operating out of fear. Help me Jesus, to trust You more and not to be afraid. Increase my faith Lord and forgive me for these sins. Thank You, God that Your Word says, when we confess our sins, You are faithful to forgive and cleanse us from all unrighteousness, so based on Your Word Lord, I receive Your forgiveness and I declare that I am forgiven. I renounce agreement with the spirits of fear and control right now, in Jesus' name and I break them off of my life, right now. I command them to leave me now and never come back. Holy Spirit, come and fill me to overflowing; saturate me in Your love and empower me to walk in love, peace, joy and faith. In Jesus' mighty name, Amen."

Beloved, bless you for walking this difficult road with me. Bless you for opening your heart and allowing me to speak some hard truths to you. All of these same things, I have had to confront in my own life at one point or another, so I understand how emotional it can be. It can feel like a rototiller digging at your heart and the exposure of things that are not so pretty can bring regret and shame. Please remember and stand on the truth, there is no condemnation for those who are in Christ Jesus. Do not let a spirit of guilt and condemnation sit on you. Rebuke it, receive forgiveness, and rise holy and righteous in His sight as you are meant to be. You are beautiful and you are loved. It's not easy to admit what's in our hearts at times, but I know without a doubt, you will experience more of God's power in your life, more of His healing, peace, and love as you are willing to open yourself up.

Just a few more crucial conversations beloved and we can move on to easier discussions and topics. Hang in there. Trust the Spirit to lead you all the way through.

Bitter Judgements & Ungodly Promises

Nineteen years ago, we were living temporarily in a foreign country and a foreign culture. Our first born, Jessica, was six years old at the time, when she needed to be in school, but rather than put her in a traditional school where everything would be new to her, we decided to home school. It worked out well. We did schoolwork in the morning and since she was the only student, we accomplished what needed to be done and then enjoyed the afternoon at the pool, on the beach or doing something fun.

What I didn't count on was how it would challenge my patience. There was a definite learning curve to being able to teach well and handle the heat when she had trouble understanding the material. One day while teaching a lesson, I lost it, and I was immediately convicted. We took a break, and I had a time out.

I was seeing in myself some very familiar behavior that my own mother exhibited when I was young. It was a behavior that hurt me, and I knew that I was now hurting Jessica in the same way, as I allowed my frustration to boil over and spew loud, angry words. I had known it was an issue for a little while, but I felt powerless to stop it. I couldn't figure out why I had such trouble with self-control when I was frustrated. I didn't want to act that way but didn't know how to change.

I sat on the sofa and prayed. As I did, I felt the Lord reveal to me that He would show me a different way of parenting. I recognized that my mom was a yeller, and I knew I was now manifesting the same thing. History was repeating itself as I made the same mistakes she did. As I prayed, confessed, repented, forgave my mom, and thanked the Lord that He could teach me how to parent differently, in my mind, an intrusive thought said in a raspy, evil tone, "But you don't know how to do anything else!" I recognized the voice immediately and knew it wasn't my own, nor was it God; it was the accuser of the brethren. I rebuked the devil and made declarations of truth from God's Word. I went up one side of the devil and down the other and roasted him good because I knew that God had spoken to me just moments before. God had already confirmed to me that He was moving on my behalf, teaching me and leading me in parenting. Any word to the contrary was NOT God.

Since then, yelling angry words and fits of rage haven't been an issue. I received breakthrough that day and the Lord plucked me out of a pattern that wanted to hold me in bondage and continue down my family line. That day, I stood up and said, "No more! I won't allow this to continue." We don't have to repeat the mistakes of our own parents, but in order to be free, we do need to make sure we're not giving the devil legal ground to cause us to do so.

Do you see patterns in your behavior as a parent with the behavior of your own parents? Are you exhibiting the same bad fruit as your parents? Anger? Outbursts of rage? Hurtful words? Manipulation? Control? Passive aggressive withholding of love? Purposefully not responding to texts out of spite? If so, don't worry. I'm going to show you how to deal with it, so it stops controlling you.

Inner Vows or Promises Made to Self
Have you ever been hurt by a parent? Did you ever know, even as a youngster, that your parents' behavior was wrong? If you answered yes, pay close attention to what's coming next.

Sometimes, when we are hurt, we end up making bitter judgements against the person that hurt us. We correctly discern that someone's behavior is wrong because we're hurt by it, but very often we take it too far and make judgements against the person. We decide the *person* is bad, not just their actions, and we look down on them.

In addition, once we make a bitter judgement against someone, sometimes we go even farther and make promises or vows to ourselves that sound something like: "I'm *never* going to do that." "I'm *never* going to treat my children like that." "I'm *never* going to be like my parents" or we promise to *always* do something or be something. "I'm *always* going to ___." It could be anything, but the problem lies in our selfish ambition and sin, thinking we can do anything in our own power, apart from God. Let's not forget Jesus' statement in John 15:5, "I am the vine; you are the branches. If you remain in me and I in you, you will bear much fruit; *apart from me you can do nothing*" (Emphasis mine).

We can also make inner vows or promises to ourselves out of fear. Maybe we have witnessed something traumatic or something traumatic has happened to us. Fear and self-protection kick in and perhaps we resolve to *never, ever* do something in the future, so we don't get hurt again or in the same way as someone else was. Again, we resolve to take care of ourselves and disregard God and His protection over us. Perhaps we even become skeptical towards God and doubt His love, mercy, and protection.

Unfortunately, in these instances we are giving the devil footholds in our lives in four areas: bitterness, judgements against others, fear, and inner vows (self-protection and willfulness). When we find ourselves acting out the bad behaviors of our parents that we have despised, it is usually any combination of the above four issues that are at play as we have given the devil legal ground to hold us in a pattern of sin.

Did you feel like you were excessively controlled as a young person by your parent(s)? Were your parents strict and oppressive? Were you bitter and rebellious as a young person? Are you now acting out the same thing with your children? Do you put heavy burdens and expectations on them to be or do certain things?

Dr. Henry Malone talks about this in his book, "Shadow Boxing." He gives a great example from his experience; it is extreme, but I share it only because it makes this situation so clear. Don't be fooled; just because your own sin pattern isn't as extreme, doesn't make it any less of an opportunity for the devil. Dr. Malone writes:

> "A grandmother once came to me seeking help. With tears in her eyes, she confessed that she was abused as a child and that she abused her three children. She was troubled by watching her adult children physically abuse her grandchildren. Often, she found herself abusing them, too. 'I can't take it any longer. You must help me,' she begged.

I asked her to share about her childhood abuse. She was the third of six children. Whenever one child did something wrong, her father punished all six of them."[3]

Dr. Malone goes on to describe the horrific abuse the children endured but I will spare you the details. He continues:

"When she was ten years old she made an inner vow. She promised herself that 'if I ever have any children, I will never do to them what Daddy does to us.' While she didn't punish them in the exact same way, she beat her children with whatever was at hand... Quickly I saw that the vow she had made had imprisoned her and set her on a track that she could not get off simply because she had judged her father. When she repented of her inner vow and asked God to forgive her for judging her father, freedom came. We broke the vow and its results ceased."[4]

Another example of how inner vows can control one's life is from my own experience. Because of different traumatic things that I experienced and witnessed as a young person, when I was about twelve years old, I made an inner vow out of fear, to *never* have children. At the age of twenty-four and twenty-five, I wasn't able to conceive. For just over a year, my husband and I tried to begin our little family, but we had no success whatsoever until one day, I said to a good friend, "Isn't it funny, when I was young, I said that I was never going to have children. Now look at me!" My friend and mentor knew the power of a vow, so she took me under her wing and ministered freedom to me. I repented and together we renounced the vow and broke the power of my words. The *very next month*, after

---

[3] Dr. Henry Malone, *Shadow Boxing* (Lewisville: Vision Life Publications, 1999), 78. Print.
[4] Malone, *Shadow Boxing*, 78. Print.

more than twelve months of no success, I was pregnant for the very first time.

Once I broke the vow and repented for being self-willed, trying to control my own future and shutting God out, the devil lost his grip and his power to hold me back. I submitted my fertility back to God's control, then His will and desire was finally able to be done in my life.

Here's what the Word of God says about judging others:

> "Do not judge, or you too will be judged. For in the same way you judge others, you will be judged, and with the measure you use, it will be measured to you. (Matthew 7:1-2)

> "Do not judge, and you will not be judged. Do not condemn and you will not be condemned. Forgive and you will be forgiven. (Luke 6:37)

> You, therefore, have no excuse, you who pass judgement on someone else, for at whatever point you judge another, you are condemning yourself, because you who pass judgement do the same things. (Romans 2:1)

These scriptures point out that we have no righteousness of our own to be able to stand in judgement of someone else. It is right that we discern right from wrong but don't ever think that we have the right to condemn someone or look down on them because of their actions. That is God's department. He is the only One who knows hearts.

Here's what the Bible says about bitterness:

> Make every effort to live in peace with everyone and to be holy; without holiness no one will see the Lord. See to it that no one falls short of the grace of God and

that no bitter root grows up to cause trouble and defile many. (Hebrews 12:14-15)

Don't allow bitterness to defile you beloved. Bitterness is a root, and many bad trees and bad fruit will grow out of it. Confess it to God, renounce it and ask the Lord to remove it from you.

Here's what the Bible says about vows:

> "Again, you have heard that it was said to the people long ago, 'Do not break your oath, but fulfill to the Lord the vows you have made.' But I tell you, do not swear an oath at all: either by heaven, for it is God's throne; or by the earth, for it is his footstool; or by Jerusalem, for it is the city of the Great King. And do not swear by your head, for you cannot make even one hair white or black. All you need to say is simply 'Yes' or 'No'; anything beyond this comes from the evil one. (Matthew 5:33-37)

Simply say "yes" or "no." In my case, rather than being obstinate and saying, "I'm never going to have children," it would have been better for me to have said, "Right now, I don't feel like I want to have children when I'm older, but regardless, let God be God over my life. I choose to trust Him and do what He wants me to." This is holy submission and surrender that always honors God.

What about you, beloved? Can you identify any bitterness in your heart? Any judgements you've made against anyone? Have you made a declaration in your heart that a certain someone certainly won't see the Lord because of what they've done? Have you made any vows out of fear, trauma, or judgement? Have you decided, "I'm *never* going to let my son marry someone like that?" Or "I'm *never* going to accept her into this family?" Or "I'm *never* going to stop being his mother?" All these statements reflect self-will and stubbornness against what God may want to do in your life and in your son's life. We must be open to what God wants to do. We must put our own will on the altar, sacrifice our fleshly desires and say, "Not my will Lord, but yours be done."

Seek the Lord and pray, confessing your bitterness, judgements, fears, and vows, then break the vows and renounce them. Receive the Lord's forgiveness and pray as you are led.

Letting Go

There's a river flowing from the throne room of God; a river of power and grace that heals and transforms all who will align themselves with Jesus. The water is thick, like oil, covering and coating, healing, and mending. It glistens like diamonds, and flows to your lowest point, bringing life and light to your soul. This is the raw power of God and by its very nature, heals everything it touches.

Remember the woman with the issue of blood? She simply touched the hem of Jesus' garment, without even His knowledge, and received a miracle. Jesus had no warning she was coming, and He made no decision to heal her. Her pure, raw faith and expectation simply drew like a magnet, the miraculous power that was on Him, and she was healed. Jesus said to her, "Daughter, your faith has healed you" (Mark 5:34).

The power of God heals and when we apprehend it, it will heal us as well. It comes to us by the Holy Spirit, when we honor, love, trust, and depend on, welcome, invite, believe, and worship Father, Son AND Holy Spirit equally, forsaking all other lovers and allowing the Holy Spirit to move, without quenching, resisting, or stifling Him. This is how we position ourselves to receive from God and His river of life.

What can block that river from reaching us? Dishonor. Resisting Holy Spirit. Quenching the movement of God. Trying to control the Holy Spirit and what He's doing; trying to contain Him; putting Him in a box, as well as the things we have been talking about thus far (if they are not surrendered to Christ): un-forgiveness, believing lies from the enemy, an orphan spirit or mentality, not knowing who we are, lack of trust in God, open wounds from the past, rejection, being angry with God, ungodly emotional ties, fear, unconfessed sin, ungodly vows, and the last and final block we will address now: Idolatry.

Idolatry is the worship of false gods or making other things or people into gods by loving them more than God Almighty. Hardcore idolatry is what the Israelites did in Exodus 32 when they took all their gold jewelry and made it into an idol, a golden calf and worshipped it. They held a festival in honor of this god and sacrificed to it.

Today, similar worship happens in different places. One such place is Hawaii. The local people in Hawaii believe in gods who control the volcanoes. They worship these gods at the volcano's site, leaving gifts of food in an attempt to appease the god so they will keep the volcano silent and dormant.

Today, the worship of earthly elements is common. Some worship the stars and the moon and others worship crystals, looking to them for spiritual enlightenment and healing power. Anytime we attribute spiritual power to anything that has been created, we are sinning against God. We are to worship the Creator, not creation. If anything has any benefit for our health, whether it be crystals or plants or essential oils, we can recognize that it has health benefits, but also recognize that it is all because of our Creator God. Worship Him and Him alone.

God was clear when He gave the very first commandment:

> "You shall have no other gods before me. "You shall not make for yourself an image in the form of anything in heaven above or on the earth beneath or in the waters below. You shall not bow down to them or worship them; for I, the Lord your God, am a jealous God, punishing the children for the sin of the parents to the third and fourth generation of those who hate me, but showing love to a thousand generations of those who love me and keep my commandments. (Exodus 20:3-6).

Perhaps this type of idolatry hasn't affected you. Maybe you haven't been lured into its grip as many have, but there's another form of idolatry that is much more subtle and prevalent and is many times overlooked. This idolatry involves simply loving someone or something else more than God.

Kyle Idleman and City on a Hill Productions has produced an excellent small group study DVD curriculum addressing this very issue called, "gods at War: The Battle for Your Heart That Will Define Your Life." The DVD series includes powerful personal testimonies from people just like you and me. In the study, Kyle identifies gods of our culture that many of us worship without even realizing it: gods of pleasure, money, sex, power and even love.

As in the previous scripture from Genesis 30, God identifies himself as a "jealous God." What does that mean? Well, it means that when we love other things or people more than we love Him, He is jealous for us. When we give our attention, affection, and adoration to idols (things or people that have become too important to us) we are being unfaithful to God and to Him, it feels like we are having an affair. You see, since we are the bride of Christ and He is our Bridegroom, He experiences betrayal just as you would if your earthly spouse were unfaithful to you.

So how do we identify idols in our hearts, the gods that are warring within us for pre-eminence, demanding our adoration and affections? It's not an easy task as Jeremiah 17:9 says, "The heart is deceitful above all things and beyond cure. Who can understand it?" We tend to live in denial, and you may even have already assumed that nothing about this conversation applies to you. I would encourage you to dig a little deeper with me and look beyond the surface of your heart.

Kyle Idleman suggests some probing questions to help us identify idols. They are:

1. What has left you feeling the most disappointed? (Being profoundly disappointed could mean something was too important to you.)

2. What do you complain about?

3. What do you sacrifice your time and money for? What has been your biggest investment? (Would you be willing to give it up if God asked you to?)

4. What do you worry about?

5. What are you the most fearful of losing?

6. Where do you go when you're hurt, and you need comfort? (What if that thing or person wasn't available? How would you feel?)

7. What makes you unreasonably mad?

8. What do you dream of? (How will you feel about God if that dream does not come to pass?)

9. Whose encouragement or approval means the most to you?[5]

I would add these questions as well:

1. What affects your self-worth? What makes you feel bad about yourself? What do you turn to, to help you feel good about yourself?

2. Is there a circumstance in your life that needs to be present for you to feel successful or secure?

In addition, fill in the blank:

"I will never be completely happy until _____."

As you've contemplated these questions, you may have been able to identify some idols in your life. I would encourage you to confess it to God, repent and ask Him to forgive you. Then, make the appropriate adjustments in your life to make sure God is on the throne of your heart and that you are not expecting Him to share it with anything or anyone else.

Promises and Dreams

As we continue, let's focus on idolatry in a few specific areas: our children and our hopes and dreams for them. We all had them, didn't we? The moment we held our child in our arms for the first time, we wanted the best for them. We wanted them to be happy their whole lives and we wanted to protect them from anything less. As they grew, we saw in them gifts and talents, strengths and abilities that could take them far in life. We envisioned for them what their futures could look like, and we were hopeful and excited, encouraging them to be all

---

[5] Kyle Idleman, *gods at War* (Louisville: City on a Hill Productions, 2012), DVD.

they could be. Perhaps putting them through college or university and working extra hours to do so. For some, the dreams we had for our children became reality. For others, they did not—at least not yet.

As our children grow into adults and find their own way, our hopes, and dreams for them may need to be released to the Lord. Holding onto them for too long may be causing more strife, stress, and hardship for you than they're worth. Perhaps it's time to release your son/daughter and your dreams to God and just trust Him and allow Him to work in their heart.

You may need to grieve. You may need to take your disappointment to God and be healed. After all, it's more important to maintain a heart connection and relationship with your children, than it is to try and force something that they don't want right now.

If you believe you've had a promise from God regarding your child's future, hold on to it, pray about it, but re-evaluate from time to time with God. If we're honest, sometimes we have difficulty discerning the difference between a promise from God and our own soulish desire. Above all, don't try to control things. Keep it close to your heart and wait. Be patient for God to work things out.

Abram from the Bible had a promise from God, but he had to wait twenty-five years to see the fulfillment of it. I bet he didn't expect that! Before Abram actually received the promise, God instructed him to pack up and take a journey, leaving his homeland behind, but God didn't actually tell him where to go. God just said to Abram, "Go from your country, your people and your father's household to the land I will show you" (Gen. 12:1). God separated Abram and set him apart from his father's house, his homeland, his ancestors, and his past, in order to accomplish His will for Abram and his descendants.

For those who like to plan, God's directive may have been a bit stressful. Ever left on a road trip not having any idea where you were going? Me neither. It appears though that Abram was not daunted by it. He packed everything and everyone up and did exactly what the Lord instructed him to do. Only as he stepped out in faith, did God direct Abram, one step at a time.

As Abram was obedient, he received a promise from God, "I will make you into a great nation and I will bless you; I will make your name great, and you will be a blessing. I will bless those who bless you, and whoever curses you I will curse; and all peoples on earth will be blessed through you" (Gen.12:2-3).

Abram was seventy-five years old when God made this first promise to him, "I will make you into a great nation," but he and his wife, Sarai, were childless. As Abram and his household travelled, God continued to speak to Abram on many occasions and made other, similar promises, promises of offspring and possessing land (Gen.12:7, Gen.13:15-16, Gen.15:4-5, Gen.15:18).

Ten years passed and I'm sure he began to wonder how and when God would act on his behalf or if maybe they were missing something. They grew impatient as any of us would, worrying that they were getting older and not understanding God's plan, so Sarai took matters into her own hands. Ever done that? She offered her maidservant, Hagar, to Abram in order to produce offspring and sure enough, they had a child. Ishmael was born when Abram was eighty-six years old, but Ishmael was not the child of promise.

God continued to speak to Abram and changed his name to Abraham and Sarai's name to Sarah. Finally, when Abraham was one hundred years old, their child of promise, Isaac, was born, twenty-five years after the first time God spoke to Abraham—twenty-five l-o-n-g years. When it was naturally and physically impossible for them to have children, God showed up and showed off, intervening on their behalf, causing them to birth Isaac together as their child of promise.

There are likely some who are reading this book who can relate in part to Abraham and Sarah's story. Indeed, you know exactly what it is like to wait a long time for God to show up on your behalf, causing your family to finally blossom. You know what it is like to finally hold your long-awaited child in your arms, and I can only imagine the fierceness of your love and protective instinct for them. For Abraham and Sarah, they longed and longed for Isaac for twenty-five years and finally they received him. How they must have spoiled him rotten! How they must have loved him and desired the best for him.

It would be very easy under these circumstances to hold on for dear life to your child, wouldn't it? Later in the story with Abraham, Sarah and Isaac, there came a time when God tested Abraham. Genesis 22:1-2 says:

> Some time later God tested Abraham. He said to him, "Abraham!" "Here I am," he replied. Then God said, "Take your son, your only son, whom you love—Isaac—and go to the region of Moriah. Sacrifice him there as a burnt offering on a mountain I will show you."

God called Abraham to put Isaac on the altar and sacrifice him. What was God testing? He was testing Abraham's obedience and his loyalties. God wanted to see if Abraham would put Him first and do as He had asked. In addition, God was establishing a new way of worship for Abraham and his family.

Abraham was obedient to the Lord and took Isaac to Mount Moriah to sacrifice him there, however, something miraculous happened just in time. Just before Abraham was about to thrust the knife into his son, an angel of the Lord called out to stop him.

> "Do not lay a hand on the boy," he said. "Do not do anything to him. Now I know that you fear God, because you have not withheld from me your son, your only son." Abraham looked up and there in a thicket he saw a ram caught by its horns. He went over and took the ram and sacrificed it as a burnt offering instead of his son. So Abraham called that place The Lord Will Provide. And to this day it is said, "On the mountain of the Lord it will be provided." (Gen. 22:12-14)

Of course, we read that story and we're horrified that God would even suggest such a thing. It's so cruel. I can't imagine how Isaac felt as he was tied up and put on the altar by his own father, however, what we don't know is the history and practices of the time. It was actually common for Abraham's ancestors to sacrifice their children to pagan gods. I know, it's hard to believe. This was a practice that the Lord hated which is why God removed Abraham from his homeland and ancestors—God separated Abraham from his father's home and sent him on a journey to a land he did not know.

I could never figure out why Abraham was so willing to do as God had instructed. It didn't appear from scripture that he second guessed himself or questioned the Lord at all. This is because Abraham was familiar with the practice of child sacrifice, but the amazing part is God showed Abraham that He, the Lord, would provide a different sacrifice acceptable to Him, in place of Isaac. God in effect was saying, *no longer, will you sacrifice your children; this is not my way. I will provide the sacrifice.*

Abraham passed the test and the Lord said to him, *"Now I know that you fear God."* Just as God wanted Abraham's heart to be solely His, so He wants our hearts to be His, as well. No long-awaited child or any hope or promise of God should ever become so important to us that it becomes more important than God himself. If God tells us to sacrifice or kill something, it's because we have elevated it up where it doesn't belong; it sits in a high place and must come down.

Is there something in your life that you would not be willing to give up for God? Is there anything in your life that is so controlling your emotions that you have no peace? Maybe it's a hope, a dream, plan, or desire. Perhaps a certain ambition, opportunity or simply security. Perhaps it's a spouse, a second chance after divorce. Whatever it is, let it go and let God fill your life with Him and His goodness. Who knows what God's goodness over your life might include? It's probably so much more than you ever thought possible.

Just as Isaac, Abraham's first descendent was spared by the sacrifice of another, a ram caught in a thicket, we too, have been spared by the sacrifice of another, Jesus Christ, the Lamb of God that takes away the sins of the world. Just as God provided a 'stand in' sacrifice for Isaac, so He did for all of us too.

Let's honour God and love Him first. Simply repent for idolatry and the blood of Jesus will come and wash you clean. "If we confess our sins, he is faithful and just and will forgive us our sins and purify us from all unrighteousness" (1 John 1:9).

I'm so glad that you have been willing to take this healing journey with me, however, do not fret about not praying perfectly, not understanding something or possibly missing something else. None of us want to "block" the blessings and healing of God in our lives and if you're like me, you want to make sure all the boxes are ticked and all the t's are crossed, however, I've got good news my friend. As long as we are willing to lay our hearts out before the Lord, He is mighty enough to remove everything that binds. Whatever the Spirit puts His finger on specifically, deal with it, then trust God with the rest.

Here's what I hear the Spirit whisper to me today. "Believe again. Yield. Trust. Surrender. Believe again, in the raw, pure, powerful, outrageous love, goodness and mercy of God to blast like dynamite through everything that hinders us, to heal us and restore us in every way!" Nothing can stop Him! He is the Way Maker—the One who can't be held back and the One whose mercy is fresh, unending, and aggressively chases us down and overtakes us, as we yield to Him.

I used to think that I had to figure it all out; to know exactly what was in my heart, stopping and blocking God. Was I still angry? Was I jealous? Was I offended? I don't know, perhaps all of it, but none of it *surrendered*, is enough to stop the all-consuming inferno of God's grace and mercy that overcomes. There is no need for us to name it, to figure it all out, to psychoanalyze—just yield, surrender, let Him in and the name that is above every other name, JESUS will BLAST through it all and burn it away. Faith. We, I, must come back to simplicity and CHILD-LIKE, pure faith that truly believes that ALL things are possible with God and that His grace is completely sufficient for ALL healing and transformation. Nothing, absolutely nothing, I have to offer is needed to add into the mix. There is no mix. It's ALL Jesus.

The Lord is showing me alabaster jars in my mind. Expensive, ornate, little jars, each corked containing something held dear, but the contents are not what one would expect. Inside these jars, perfectly painted with human hands, crafted by works of the flesh, lay memories; memories of events, un-surrendered, un-yielded, held onto... Not because the memories are good, but because they were impactful, life-altering, not easily forgotten, and earned. We've earned the right to hang onto the jars after all we've been through.

It's time—it's time to do as Mary did. It is time to surrender and pour them out onto the nail scarred feet of Jesus and watch the contents of our suffering be transformed into precious and holy oil, uncorked, uncapped, and yielded to Christ. May our memories and pain not be bottled up but poured out. May our hearts be surrendered and open, displayed on an Alabaster plate—not closed up in little jars in pieces and parcels. May we be willing to allow Christ to access it ALL, to take away at His will, to transform and replace, whenever He sees fit with His wonderful mercy and life-changing, transforming love.

Where are your alabaster jars? What do they contain? Take a deep breath, oh brave one! Break them open. Pour them out. Anoint His feet and be healed.

Prodigals

As I sit down to write and form the words on this page, I'm getting excited as I know I'm nearing the finish line. Part of me just wants to rush through it and get it done, but I know that the best books are the ones that come from deep contemplation and the anointing of the Holy Spirit. If you've ever written a book, you know it's a labor of love; it's always more than you thought, and it always takes longer than you expect. So, I will put on my patience and wait for the right and strategically appointed words to come, as this chapter was not in the original plan. There is something on God's heart right now that needs to be communicated.

Many of you reading this book have had hopes and dreams for your son. You envisioned him as a pastor, a preacher, a missionary or at the very least, a passionate follower of God, but that has not come to be. You've been praying and that is good, but you've also been stressing, worrying and fearful, but beloved, that is not God's will for you. I pray that in the previous chapter, you've been able to put those hopes and dreams on the altar and give them to God. Remember His Word to us in Proverbs 3:5-8:

> Trust in the Lord with all your heart and lean not on your own understanding; in all your ways submit to him, and he will make your paths straight. Do not be wise in your own eyes; fear the Lord and shun evil. This will bring health to your body and nourishment to your bones.

Many of those same sons, the ones that have been held so close, have caused pain and great disappointment in the hearts of their moms and those same moms have wondered, *what did I do wrong?*

The Lord would say to you:

> "Daughter, do not fret and do not worry. Do not presume that you are to blame. Rest in the knowledge that I am with you, and I have not left your son's side, but I am working behind the scenes to accomplish all that I have planned. Nothing is too difficult for me and no heart too hard. My arm reacheth to the depths of the deepest pit and rescues those fallen deep in the mire. There is nothing too difficult for me. Get ready. Get ready; for you will see what you never expected, and you will hear what you never thought you'd hear, coming from the mouths of the ones once scattered. Open your heart and get ready. Forgive the prodigals, forgive the lost, forgive the wayward; forgive their words, forgive their actions, forgive their mistakes, forgive their sin. Forgive beloved, and you will receive the best I have for you."

In August of this year (2019), I was cut to the heart after hearing of two mass shootings that took place over the span of one weekend: one shooting in Dayton, Ohio and one in El

Paso, Texas. I was led by God to write an article entitled, "It's Always the Boy," which I believe I am to include in this book (see Appendix B, pg. 115) and also began a group on Facebook called, "Shaping the Hearts of Our Sons." You are welcome to join us there. I would like to share with you my post from September 15, 2019:

This is what I hear the Spirit of God say today regarding families:

"It's not over until I say it's over!" Many are discouraged with the division and lack of connection in their families, between fathers and sons and mothers and sons, sometimes due to persecution and sometimes just due to misunderstandings—twisted words and twisted beliefs. Due to this discouragement, many have said, "It's over. I'll never get him back," but the Spirit says:

> "It's NOT over till I say, it's over and I'm not saying it's over. I'm saying, it's only begun. The softening and reconciliation of your hearts, and the truth coming forth to heal, has only begun. Get ready to see what you thought would never happen. Get ready to see the great 'coming home.' Watch for it and be ready to shift, to forgive, to move as I move; fling wide the doors and receive that which I have released."

Be encouraged my friend. The Lord sees your heart and your concerns. He sees your angst and how much you miss your son. He is working on your behalf, and He wants your family reunited just as much as you do. He will see the Lord. They, all those in your family who are not lined up, will see the Lord. The time is coming when the Spirit will be poured out like never before; miracles, signs and wonders will break lose and the minds of the doubters will be opened. Pray beloved and declare the veil over your son's (and everyone in your family who doesn't yet believe) understanding is torn and removed from his mind and his spiritual eyes, in Jesus' mighty name. The 'great coming home' is coming beloved. Wait and watch for it; just as the father in the parable of the prodigal son waited and watched for his son, wait, and watch for yours as well. Lastly, prepare your heart now to forgive and to receive him. Be in a position to bless him when he crosses back over the threshold of your home crying out for mercy in the fear of the Lord.

Releasing and Sending

Hannah, one of the many mothers in the Bible that I admire and want to emulate, was faithful, sacrificial and she loved and trusted God. In first Samuel 2:1-2, Hannah sang to the Lord:

> "My heart rejoices in the Lord; in the Lord my horn is lifted high. My mouth boasts over my enemies, for I delight in your deliverance. "There is no one holy like the Lord; there is no one besides you; there is no Rock like our God.

Hannah was rejoicing, but not too long before this, her prayer sounded much different as she wept bitterly to the Lord. She was one of two wives of Elkanah, but unfortunately, Hannah was not able to conceive. Each year when they went up to Shiloh to make their sacrifice, Hannah was confronted with the harsh reality of being childless, as she watched Penninah with her children until one year. . . everything shifted.

In Hannah's desperation, she prayed to the Lord a prayer she had never prayed before. In years prior, Hannah had only wanted a baby, but this year she wept and cried out to God, moving past her own desires and into God's heart; her will finally aligned fully with His.[6]

Eli, the priest and his two sons, were not honoring the Lord well in their service, so God was looking for one to take their place. God needed a man whose heart was fully His and a man through whom He could speak; God needed a prophet to bring the Word of the Lord to the people, without compromise, so He closed Hannah's womb, and prepared her to make a great sacrifice. Finally, the time came; her heart became hungry enough to walk out what God had planned and she made a vow to the Lord:

> "LORD Almighty, if you will only look on your servant's misery and remember me, and not forget your servant but give her a son, then I will give him to the LORD for all the days of his life, and no razor will ever be used on his head." (1 Samuel 1:11)

Hannah's submission and surrender were exactly what God needed and she was finally positioned to be blessed. Shortly after, Hannah found herself pregnant and later gave birth to a son named Samuel.

After she had weened Samuel, she made good on her promise to the Lord and took him to the temple to be raised by Eli, as a servant of God. Such a sacrifice! God honored her and was faithful to Hannah; she gave her first born back to the Lord and He gave her five more children, three sons and two daughters (1 Samuel 2:21).

---

[6] Jane Hansen, "A New Season," *God's Bold Call to Women*, Ed. Barbara J. Yoder. (Ventura: Regal Books, 2005) 101. Print.

Samuel was called to be a prophet, living apart from his mother and family, being raised by the priest. The Lord was with Samuel, causing him to have favor and his words to have influence. Just as Hannah honored the call on Samuel's life, we too must honor the call on our son's life. It may be a sacrifice for us, but God is calling us to be faithful to His purposes and to align with His will, just like Hannah did.

What does your son's call look like? In these last days, some will be called to the nations, laboring and working for the Lord to bring in the harvest. They may have to travel. They may have to be far away from family. Will you release him? Will you allow him to be sent? Will you bless him as he goes?

Just as you are the bride of Christ, called to shine with the glory of God in your own unique way, so is he. He may start out in the marketplace or the corporate world somewhere close, but God could be preparing him for more. Your son, living and breathing now on purpose, will be part of the end time church; he could be called out as a remnant, set apart for God to do great exploits for Him. It's going to be messy; Isaiah 60:2 confirms it. It may not be comfortable, and it may be risky. He may be sent into hostile places or nations closed to the gospel, but will you trust God? Will you get out of the way and let God be God in your son's life?

There's a meme on social media I love: "Your greatest contribution to the Kingdom of God may not be something you do, but someone you raise." So much is in your hands; you can restrict and be an obstacle or you can release and be a blessing. The choice is yours.

Ephesians 2:10 says, "For we are God's handiwork, created in Christ Jesus to do good works, which God prepared in advance for us to do." There is work that the Lord has assigned to you and your offspring. With all love and compassion, I implore you, let's get to work and let's release our sons to do their part with God in His Kingdom. Other people's lives could depend on it and there could be someone right now, waiting on your obedience.

What Now?

Congratulations beloved—you've made it through all my probing and *in your face* questions. I hope we can still be friends. I also hope and pray you've been able to uncover some keys to restoring peace in your heart and rest in your heavenly Father's love, but now it's time to make sure you don't fall back into a destructive emotional pattern. Moving forward, it would be healthy to make some changes in your routine and begin to create a new groove in your mind and life.

What's next? Here are some ideas for you to consider:

1. Continue to release your son emotionally and commit him to the Lord daily. I don't believe this is a one-time deal, but this may have to be done daily for a while, at least until your emotions line up with your will.

2. Continue to seek emotional healing and wholeness for your own heart. Pray and ask the Lord to direct you in this and make sure to spend some time in solitude with Him.

Make space for the Holy Spirit to move. Pick up my book, "Position Yourself for Healing" from Amazon and work through it. You could also get help from a professional counsellor if need be.

3. Seek the Lord daily. If you don't have a routine of a daily quiet time with the Lord, begin one. Read the Word, pray and listen to the Lord. Grow in intimacy with Him.

4. Journal. You could journal during your quiet times, and you could also do some self-reflection. See Appendix C, page 123, for some great questions to get you thinking and looking into your heart.

5. Fast for spiritual breakthrough. Fasting food (or certain types of food) allows you to direct your hunger and cravings toward God and forces you to get your needs met by Him. This creates an opportunity to receive amazing revelation and understanding. You could do a Daniel fast or a water fast (always check with your doctor first) or ask the Lord what He would want you to fast. Perhaps it's just sweets or something else, like Facebook or the internet.

6. Worship in a new way. Do something risky, something you've not done before. Lift your hands to Him. Lift BOTH your hands to Him, straight up, ALL THE WAY. Jump, shout, and get loud if you must—just do something new.

7. Continue to forgive those who hurt you. Forgive your husband as often as needed. Ask the Lord to show you who and for what.

8. Pray the scriptures.

9. Pray for your son and declare scriptures over him. Declare Psalm 91 over him for protection.

10. Mend or restore your relationship with your husband. Remember how you felt when you were first married. Go to the places you used to when you were in love. Listen to the music you used to listen to. Go for a weekend getaway together. Choose to love again and have some fun together.

11. Find new friendships with like-minded women.

12. Join a Bible study group at your church. If you don't have a church, find one.

13. Serve at your church or volunteer somewhere.

14. Discover what you're passionate about. Do some soul searching to figure this out. Write it down. Pray and ask the Lord where He wants you to focus your time, talents, and energy.

15. Discover your spiritual gifts and what you really enjoy doing. Maybe it's even time to write a book!

You're in a new season beloved and this season will be beautiful, just like all your previous seasons, as God is orchestrating it and He will be in it. Being a natural mother is wonderful and an honor but is very much seasonal in intensity as your children become adults. Being a spiritual mother, on the other hand, is a lifetime assignment requiring your attention and commitment every day. In Matthew 28:18-20, Jesus says to His disciples:

> "All authority in heaven and on earth has been given to me. Therefore go and make disciples of all nations, baptizing them in the name of the Father and of the Son and of the Holy Spirit, and teaching them to obey everything I have commanded you. And surely I am with you always, to the very end of the age."

Mark 16:15-18 expands on what Jesus said with this:

> "Go into all the world and preach the gospel to all creation. Whoever believes and is baptized will be saved, but whoever does not believe will be condemned. And these signs will accompany those who believe: In my name they will drive out demons; they will speak in new tongues; they will pick up snakes with their hands; and when they drink deadly poison, it will not hurt them at all; they will place their hands on sick people, and they will get well."

We are all called to love others as Christ loved us and participate in the expansion of the Kingdom of God, in whatever way the Lord has gifted us and equipped us: preaching, writing, being a living testimony somehow, even healing the sick, casting out demons and doing all that Jesus did and more, using Godly wisdom, not putting the Lord to the test, but following His lead wherever He goes. We are to participate with the Lord in what He is doing, so beloved, ask the Lord to open your eyes to what He is doing around you, and join Him there. It is time to rise and move into the more that God has for you.

When Christ returns, only those shining as they were called to shine will be invited into the wedding feast; those with their lamps dim and going out, will miss it. In the parable of the ten virgins from Matthew 25, each blood-washed one, was required to have their own lamp and each lamp had to be burning with the oil of intimacy and obedience. There will be no sharing of lamps when Christ returns. We will not be able to ride on anyone's coat tail or hitch a ride with anyone else's faith, so be ready with the lamp of the Holy Spirit within you, the oil of intimacy, obedience and faith stored up and the fire of God burning brightly.

As this season fades, embrace your new roles, responsibilities and assignments with faith, grace, and the power of God. Be healed, be bold, be courageous and be all that God created you to be.

Thank you once again for giving me the privilege of speaking into your life and trusting me with your heart. May you be led through the valley with peace, straight through to the other side, discovering the joy of the Lord in unlikely places and may the goodness and great mercies of our God surround you, strengthen you and bless you now and always.

Thank you to God for His outpouring of wisdom, grace, and insight onto the pages of this book. May He use it for His glory. Amen.

Appendix A

Welcome! I'm so glad you have turned to this page! It can only mean one thing; you have decided, for the very first time to repent and invite the Lord Jesus to come into your life as your very own Lord and Savior. When we decide to surrender to Jesus, it is the work of the Holy Spirit. He is the one that draws us to Himself, and He is the One who convicts us of our sin, so I will not be giving you a neat little prayer to recite. I will leave it up to the Holy Spirit to guide you, but first, here are some key scriptures to read:

> Romans 3:23 says, "for all have sinned and fall short of the glory of God,"
>
> 1 John 1:8-9 says, "If we claim to be without sin, we deceive ourselves and the truth is not in us. If we confess our sins, he is faithful and just and will forgive us our sins and purify us from all unrighteousness."
>
> Romans 6:23 says, "For the wages of sin is death, but the gift of God is eternal life in Christ Jesus our Lord."
>
> John 3:3 says, "Jesus replied, 'Very truly I tell you, no one can see the kingdom of God unless they are born again.'"
>
> John 14:6 says, "Jesus answered, 'I am the way and the truth and the life. No one comes to the Father except through me.'"
>
> Romans 10:9-11 says, "If you declare with your mouth, 'Jesus is Lord,' and believe in your heart that God raised him from the dead, you will be saved. For it is with your heart that you believe and are justified, and

it is with your mouth that you profess your faith and are saved. As Scripture says, 'Anyone who believes in him will never be put to shame.'"

Ephesians 2:8-9, "For it is by grace you have been saved, through faith—and this is not from yourselves, it is the gift of God—not by works, so that no one can boast."

Acts 2:38-39 says, "Peter replied, 'Repent and be baptized, every one of you, in the name of Jesus Christ for the forgiveness of your sins. And you will receive the gift of the Holy Spirit. The promise is for you and your children and for all who are far off—for all whom the Lord our God will call.'"

Jesus says in Revelation 3:20, "Here I am! I stand at the door and knock. If anyone hears my voice and opens the door, I will come in and eat with that person, and they with me."

He's calling you my friend, back home into His arms. In order to receive the gift of eternal life you will need to make a series of sincere choices. First you will need to be utterly convinced that you need God, that you can't do *anything* more without Him. Then you can choose to:

- ❖ Repent – which means to change your mind and to change direction; to turn from your own way to God's way.

- ❖ Agree with God that you have sinned and fallen short of His glory.

- ❖ Confess your sin to God.

- ❖ Believe that Jesus Christ is the Son of God and that He rose from the dead.

- ❖ Surrender your life to Christ and commit to follow His ways.
- ❖ Declare with your mouth, "Jesus Christ is Lord."
- ❖ Thank God for His faithfulness and forgiveness.

That's it my friend! Pray right now, share your heart with God making sure to cover these points.

Once you do this sincerely, from your heart, you are officially part of the family of God! You are born again *by the Spirit of God*; the Holy Spirit has brought you back to life and He has taken up residence within you. You now have direct access through Jesus to God, our heavenly Father and He welcomes you into the throne room. As you seek God and get to know Him through reading His Word, He will begin to change your heart and your desires so that they align with His. Don't get down on yourself if you don't do everything exactly right; God is gracious and most forgiving. He's not a harsh task master and He's not angry with you or ready to punish you at every turn.

Here's a few next steps that I would recommend (in addition to reading the rest of this book!):

- ❖ Get a Bible and begin reading in the book of John. Get a version that is easy to read such as: The New International Version, New American Standard Bible or New Living Translation. If you use an app first on your phone, you can check out many different versions and decide which one you like best (biblegateway.com is a good site/app).
- ❖ Ask Jesus to baptize you in the Holy Spirit and invite the Holy Spirit to completely fill you.
- ❖ Tell God about your trials and invite Him into the midst of them.

Appendix A | 143

- ❖ Ask God for direction from His Word.
- ❖ Pray and fellowship with God daily.
- ❖ Look for God's activity in your life and thank Him for it.
- ❖ Ask God what church you should attend. He will lead you to a church that teaches from the Bible and teaches a full gospel.
- ❖ Get baptized in water at the church you decide to attend.
- ❖ Seek out other believers who are like-minded, encouraging, and supportive.
- ❖ Trust God to guide you and to answer your prayers in a way that is best for you.
- ❖ Let peace in your spirit be a guide for you.

That's it! Congratulations again and God bless you as you forge ahead on your path of faith, with Christ in you, before you and all around you.

Now, turn back to page 17 and enjoy the rest of the book.

Appendix B

It's Always the Boy

Oh, I'm agonizing over that title. Am I pointing fingers? Am I blaming? It may sound like it, but that is not my intent. My intent is to speak the truth and to call out what's going on right before our eyes. The truth is... It *IS* always a boy. There's no way around it. It's politically incorrect and some would say, downright sexist, but before something can be dealt with, we need to be real and be willing to say the difficult things. It's almost never a girl—herein lies a major key to begin to unravel one of the most common, yet heinous crimes in many nations today.

What am I talking about? I'm talking about the incomprehensible evil that is causing a segment of the male population to stand in public places and unleash multiple rounds of ammunition in a school or into a crowd, killing as many innocent bystanders as possible—whomever is in the way, including children. I'm talking about the violence, the hopelessness and even abandonment that has gripped the minds and actions of some young men, causing them to act out in a way that, dare I say, has become commonplace for them.

Yes, there are many factors at play here. We cannot blame just one thing alone. Sometimes there's political stances involved, sometimes there's not. But I believe now we have reached a point of desperation. A few weeks ago, there were two mass shootings in one weekend: El Paso, Texas and Dayton, Ohio. We must begin to address the factors involved. It is not enough simply to pray. Prayer is necessary—the beginning point and also the foundation for all that follows, but we must move now, into action. It is time to put action to our faith and begin to partner with God in the breaking of this evil scheme of the devil. As I have prayed around this issue, I believe that the Lord has shown me that a sense of abandonment is a large *part* of what's fueling this behavior.

Indeed, right now, I call $EVERY$ parent to action. Every parent and every adult on the face of this God loving planet has a part to play. Do you remember that phrase from days gone by? That phrase from the days that were simpler and recognized the power of community?

It takes a village.

Yeah, that one. Remember that? There was GREAT wisdom there. It takes a village my friends, to raise children well and whole so they become competent members of society, making the contribution they were designed for. We cannot do this on our own. We must rely on each other to help, to advise, to come along side, to watch and to pray for one another. We must stop our prideful arrogance, believing and insisting on doing things our own way; not listening to anyone else or receiving what they have to offer. We must open ourselves up to others and the Godly wisdom they have, and we must NOW, open ourselves up to God again and seek for His direction in this matter. So, what's the plan of action?

First, let's realize that no parent ever thinks that their son would ever do such a thing; no parent would ever say, "I think my son might be the next mass shooter". They may *see* and recognize that their son appears depressed or distant, disconnected, and angry at times, but never do they think that they would resort to such behavior. "They know better," "Only a monster would do that, and my son is NO monster." Actually, you know what? It doesn't take a monster.

It *doesn't* take a monster.

All it takes is an emotionally *disturbed* individual, *overwhelmed* with frustration, anger, rage, *desperation*, hopelessness, and isolation; testosterone coursing through their veins, possibly an *established pattern* of venting their anger through violent video games resulting in desensitization, possibly drugs and finally, easy, legal access to a firearm. That's it. That, right there, is a recipe for disaster. No parent expects it, and every parent of every mass shooter is blindsided by it. So, what's my point? Let's open our eyes and be proactive now before it happens in our own families and before scores more people are injured or killed.

I am aware that some may think that this issue is all about gun laws but it's not. Family and mental health have much more to do with it than anything else and it's about time we talk about it. It must stop. What is going wrong or what is **missing** for boys in their families and upbringing that makes them feel disconnected, angry, unloved, and possibly unseen? Fathers? Support? Understanding? Security? A listening ear? Compassion? A safe place? Healthy boundaries? All of the above?

At the end of this past July, I found myself randomly reflecting on how different my daughter was from my boys, as we raised them through their teenage years. We have four children—one girl who is the oldest and three boys—one twenty-two-year-old and twin boys who are seventeen. Our daughter experienced some stress and anxiety through high school but was always obvious about it and willing to talk; she was expressive, and we were never in the complete dark about how she felt. When she was upset, she drew deeper into relationship with us to find comfort.

Our boys have been and are different. Around puberty, they got quieter, less interactive, preferring to spend time by themselves in their bedrooms. They came home from school and when I asked how their day was, they said "boring" or "fine" and wouldn't elaborate unless asked more specific questions. When they were stressed and anxious, they kept to themselves. They're still quiet and if my husband or I don't purposefully connect with them and encourage them to express themselves, they stay quiet. If they're hurting, they suffer in silence. They don't reach out so we must reach out to them.

Disconnection is dangerous and eventually boys will look to something or someone else for comfort or use something to try and escape from the emotional stress; for some, this could be sports, which isn't horrible, but it also could be something more damaging like violent video games or even drugs. Whatever it is, stress ends up being internalized and toxic emotions fester affecting their mental health.

Unfortunately, parents think that silence and disconnection are normal for boys and they just let it happen. *Boys don't want to talk, and boys are not emotional;* these are assumptions that parents make and frankly, we're relieved to finally have some space to ourselves, but embracing disconnect is a mistake. Boys *are* different from girls. Generally speaking, boys are more active, more aggressive, engage in high-risk behavior and many times don't think about the consequences of their actions. It's all about the moment and the adrenaline in their veins. Boys are different than girls. The testosterone that floods their bodies at puberty causes physiological changes in their brain. They are not able to identify their feelings as quickly as a girl, but they are still emotional and spiritual beings.[7] Their hearts are just as big and tender, as the girls'. They are just as affected by neglect, rejection, bullying and trauma.

Not coincidentally, the weekend after I was reflecting on these things, the shootings in El Passo and Dayton happened. I was angry and frustrated and frankly didn't really want to put the

---

[7] Dobson, *Bringing Up Boys,* 19-20. Print.

same old "Praying for El Paso" or "Praying for Dayton" message on my social media feed—it felt trite and meaningless. Then, a few days later, I was on a conference call with a women's group and our leader who lives near Dayton, told us how her son knew the shooter and that she and her community were really grieving. She needed prayer... and I was the one asked to pray for her on the call. This Canadian mom, who originally wanted to distance herself from it all, was asked to invest her heart into this issue once again. So out of love for my friend, I did. I haven't been able to let it go since.

We MUST DO something. Something NEEDS to change.

We must love our boys better.

If I may, I'd like to present to you some action points for all of us to take.

1. Every person with breath in their lungs, stop assuming that you are not at least part of the solution. Get involved. Know your own children; know your neighbors, know your friend's kids, know your kid's friends, know the kids at your church. Become a mentor to a young person; especially those who don't have two parent families. Become an adult sponsor for the youth group at your church. Share your heart and speak words of encouragement and healing to them. They need to know that they are loved, seen, and heard and that their lives matter.

2. Cry out to God for wisdom, help and insight into things that are not obvious in the natural world and easily seen with our natural eyes. Recognize when God is giving us insight and stop disregarding the internal alarm bells. Some may balk at my statements in this article, but I am

communicating this to you because I am compelled to speak by the Spirit of God.

3. Every parent: establish a *heart connection* with your children when they are young; maintain a heart connection with them as they grow into adulthood—especially the boys who tend to become quiet in adolescence and tend to disconnect. A heart connection is one of mutual love, honor and respect— it's a connection that truly believes in the love from the other person that is born through authenticity, understanding, compassion, empathy, time spent and appropriate expressions of love (physical touch, a hand on the shoulder, a hug, words of affirmation, praise and admitting when you're wrong, sharing your heart). It's a connection that is characterized by enduring and complete trust that the other person has their best interest at heart.

4. Find a good, biblical church where there is support for families. Begin taking your children when they are young and make it part of your weekly routine. That way, when they reach adolescence, they will be connected with a good group of kids having good clean fun together. They will have support from youth pastors and leaders, and you will also have support in parenting. Take advantage of prayer ministry if needed.

5. Maintain open lines of communication and honesty with your children. They need to know that you're not going to *freak out* when they admit something to you, and they need to know that you are being honest with them too—if you *model* this to them they are more likely to do it as well. Admit to them when you are wrong and ask for their forgiveness when you mess up. Children are more likely to *do* what you *do*, rather than do as they are told. As they grow, give them appropriate space to make their own *age-*

appropriate decisions. Don't be controlling and overbearing. Don't make every interaction a lecture! Let them share their ideas with you. Don't criticize them and don't under any circumstances humiliate them in front of others. Know when to back off and when to interfere. Share your heart and your concern for them.

6. Be a good role model for your children. If you act out in anger and lack self-control, they will do the same. Get help for your own needs and live Godly lives. Let your children see you read your Bible and pray. Pray over your children and bless them. Live what you preach. Adhere to the FULL counsel of God; not just the easy parts that don't require sacrifice.

7. Maintain age-appropriate boundaries. Be the parent (the one in charge) in your relationship with your children. Children need to be told *no* from time to time, when appropriate.

8. If your son withdraws, do not follow suit; do not withdraw from him. Respect his privacy and give him space, but do not withdraw and allow him to isolate. Pull him in gently but persistently. Remind him, he is loved and affirm who he is. Recognize when your son needs more help, beyond what you can provide and get it for him: prayer ministry, professional counselling, and if needed, medication.

9. Make time for family on a regular basis. Spend quality and quantity time together, even if it's just being at home with them. There's this lie I've heard that states, *it's only quality time that matters.* Not true! Children need quantity time as well. Do whatever you can to be home with your children as much as possible. Children need stability and need to feel safe.

10. Shield your boys from the culture of violence that is so pervasive in society, for as long as possible. Don't allow

them to watch violent movies and don't allow them to play violent video games. Parents need to be diligent to police what they are playing and watching, at home and at the homes of friends.

11. Don't allow computers in their bedrooms (or if you do, insist on an open-door policy) and enforce the surrender of their cell phone at bedtime. Parents need to be parents again; set the rules and enforce them whether they like it or not. If you have nurtured a heart connection with your children in an attitude of love and respect from early on, they will be more apt to accept your rules and follow them. When establishing rules, allow them to have a say, but make sure you are the one with the final authority.

12. Finally, get some resources to help you make wise choices as parents. "Bringing Up Boys" by Dr. James Dobson, "Boundaries with Kids" by Dr. Henry Cloud and Dr. John Townsend are both great resources. As well, "Have a New Kid by Friday" and "Have a New Teenager by Friday" by Dr. Kevin Leman are also good. As I find other good resources, I will pass the information on to you.

We all need to do our part in raising emotionally healthy boys and getting help for the ones who need it. Perhaps your boy(s) is/are still young, and you can implement these strategies with success. That's great. On the other hand, if your son is older and he is exhibiting anger and an unwillingness to open up to you, I would suggest humbling yourself and saying you're sorry for however you may have hurt him in the past. I know that for some parents this can seem strange but at this point, compassion and understanding, recognizing their pain, and exhibiting grace towards them is the only answer. Avoid lecturing them or criticizing them. If you're not aware of anything that you may have done to hurt them, you can say something like, "I can see that you're hurting, and I'm sorry that you're in pain. I'd like to help if I can. I'm sorry if I've done something to hurt you. I'm sorry if I haven't communicated my love to you very well. I DO love you. Please tell me what's going on so we can talk about it." As always, seek help from a professional when necessary.

I invite you to join the closed group on Facebook called *Shaping the Hearts of Our Sons,* so we can gather as a village and pray for one another, ask questions, learn from one another, and share our successes. It is vital now more than ever that we are effective at nurturing the emotional needs of our boys so that they can grow into men that love well, take responsibility, assert themselves appropriately, exercise compassion and forgiveness and empathize with others.

God bless and I hope to see you in the group.

Questions for Further Reflection

Who are you?

What are your roles in life?

Do you feel loved? If so, by whom? If not, why not?

Did you feel loved by your parents?

Do you feel loved by God?

How do you receive love? What has made you feel loved?

What could your loved ones do differently to help you feel more loved?

How do you know when there is something you should be working on with God, about yourself?

What makes you happy?

What agitates you?

What are you most afraid of losing?

What are the bad fruits in your life?

When have you experienced the intimate presence of God? What happened? How did you know it was God?

When have you felt God's absence?

When has God been silent?

What circumstances in your life can you see God moving in?

What were the formative moments that have shaped your faith in God?

What were the formative moments that have shaped who you are right now?

What is an adult son's responsibility to his mother? Perhaps discuss this with a group of women and notice if there is a difference of opinion? If there is, why do you think that is?

How does it make you feel when your adult son doesn't connect with you for a few days? For a week or more? Why do you think that is?

Do you need to know where your adult son is all the time? If so, why?

Are you proud of your son? If so, have you told him that lately? If not, why not?

If you're not proud of him, why not?

Do you see your son as a success or a failure? Why?

How do you think God sees your son?

What is God inviting you into?

What promises of God are giving you hope for the future?

About the Author

Barbara is passionate lover of Jesus and spiritual mentor who has been pursuing Jesus and the Kingdom of God for more than 30 years. With the Lord moving powerfully in her, she has experienced victory over barrenness, physical issues, and emotional strongholds that have threatened to control her life and is now imparting the same victory to others. Her passion is to share the love and power of God to heal from the inside out, through prayer and deliverance with all who will receive.

With a solid foundation on the Bible, the infallible Word of God and established fruit in her life, Barbara moves in the gifts of healing, discerning of spirits and prophecy for the encouragement of all and the equipping of the Saints. Barbara's other books, *Key to Fertility*, *Barren No More*, and *Position Yourself for Healing* are available on Amazon.

Barbara attends a Pentecostal church and makes her home near Windsor, Ontario, Canada with her husband and children.

Barbara is the founder of Destined International Kingdom Ministries providing resources and prophetic encouragement to help you shine bright and advance forward into your Kingdom call. Visit www.destined.international to read her occasional blog and follow her on Facebook at facebook.com/barbaradesimonbooks/ and Instagram at instagram.com/authorbarbaradesimon.

Bibliography

Bevere, John. *The Holy Spirit – An Introduction*. Palmer Lake, Colorado: Messenger International, 2013.

Dobson, Dr. James. *Bringing Up Boys – Practical advice and encouragement for those shaping the next generation of men*. Carol Stream, Illinois: Tyndale Momentum, 2001.

Garlough Brown, Sharon. *Sensible Shoes – A Story About the Spiritual Journey*. Downers Grove, Illinois: Intervarsity Press, 2013.

Hanson, Jane. "A New Season." *God's Bold Call to Women*. Ed. Barbara J. Yoder. Ventura, California: Regal Books, 2005.

Idleman, Kyle. *gods at War: The Battle for Your Heart That Will Define Your Life*. Louisville, Kentucky: City on a Hill Productions, 2012. DVD.

Malone, Dr. Henry. *Shadow Boxing*. Lewisville, Texas: Vision Life, 1999.

Munger, Robert Boyd. *My Heart – Christ's Home*. Downers Grove, Illinois: Intervarsity Press, 2010.

Sheets, Dutch. *Intercessory Prayer*. Ventura, California: Regal Books, 1996.

www.ingramcontent.com/pod-product-compliance
Lightning Source LLC
Chambersburg PA
CBHW022116040426
42450CB00006B/719